S0-FBV-385

Augsburg Seminary
Library
WITHDRAWN

FASCISM

AND

NATIONAL SOCIALISM

THE MACMILLAN COMPANY
NEW YORK · BOSTON · CHICAGO · DALLAS
ATLANTA · SAN FRANCISCO

MACMILLAN & CO., Limited
LONDON · BOMBAY · CALCUTTA
MELBOURNE

THE MACMILLAN COMPANY
OF CANADA, Limited
TORONTO

FASCISM
AND
NATIONAL SOCIALISM

*A Study of the Economic and Social Policies
of the Totalitarian State*

BY

MICHAEL T. FLORINSKY, Ph.D.

ASSOCIATE IN ECONOMICS
COLUMBIA UNIVERSITY

NEW YORK
THE MACMILLAN COMPANY
1936

1 8818

Copyright, 1936, by
THE MACMILLAN COMPANY.

All rights reserved—no part of this book may be
reproduced in any form without permission in writing
from the publisher, except by a reviewer who wishes
to quote brief passages in connection with a review
written for inclusion in magazine or newspaper.

Set up and printed.
Published January, 1936.

SET UP BY BROWN BROTHERS LINOTYPERS
PRINTED IN THE UNITED STATES OF AMERICA
BY THE FERRIS PRINTING COMPANY

JC
481
F55

PREFACE

IT WOULD seem almost inevitable that a student of Russian Bolshevism should yield sooner or later to the temptation to examine the ideas and institutions of Fascism and National Socialism. In spite of the open hostility that exists between the U.S.S.R., on the one hand, and Fascist Italy and National Socialist Germany, on the other, there are striking similarities between them; similarities that lie perhaps not so much in the principles as in the methods of the two antagonistic systems. Intellectual curiosity sometimes works with greater precision than does economic determinism. I have long been interested in the Soviet Union, in the evolution of Communist ideas and of the economic institutions of the proletarian State. In the end this has led me to embark upon a more intensive examination of the experiments that are being conducted in Italy and Germany. The present book is the outcome of this intellectual adventure. The task has been a fascinating one, but it has also been one full of pitfalls and dangers. An obvious difficulty that the student of Fascism and National Socialism has to face is presented by the processes of continuous remodelling at work in the institutions of Italy and Germany. Although in Italy Fascism has been in control for thirteen years the Corporate State is still

18818

far from completion. Under the pressure of necessity and of changing ideas it has been subjected to
endless readjustments, significant departures from
the original blueprints which were never very clear.
Will the Corporate State of today, assuming that it
survives the test of time and the buffetings of the
political tempest now raging over Europe and Africa,
be in the future more like the ideal for which Mussolini is striving than are the present institutions
of the Soviet Union like those of the ideal classless
and stateless community of the Communist dreams?
The question may well be asked.

What is true of Italy is even more so of Germany
where the National Socialist State is just entering
upon its fourth year. The work of reorganization,
whatever we may think of its intrinsic value, that
has been done by the Hitler Government in this
brief period is truly amazing. It seems certain that
much of it is of a merely provisional nature, again
assuming that National Socialism withstands the
test of time. In spite of these obvious and substantial limitations certain principles underlying both
the Italian and the German structures and some important outlines of the structure itself emerge with
a reasonable degree of clarity. An attempt to grasp
and describe them may not be entirely useless.

The second and even more formidable difficulty is
the inescapable fact that Fascism and National
Socialism—the latter especially—are among the
burning problems of the day. The atmosphere of
political passion that at present envelops Italy and

Germany confuses the issues, obscures one's judgment, and makes anything but easy that attitude of serenity and objectivity which is the very essence of a scientific investigation. The ability to understand the point of view of other people, even when one does not share it, is in my opinion the only real criterion of culture. By that criterion I have tried to govern myself in this study. This does not mean, of course, that I have refrained from criticism or from expressing my own views. What I have tried to do however is to interpret the Fascist and National Socialist policies not only from *our,* but also from *their* respective points of view. To what extent I have succeeded it is not for me to judge.

My knowledge of Germany goes back to pre-war days. Since the war I have several times returned to Germany; in 1932, a few months before the Nazi Revolution, again in 1934 in connection with a study I was then making of the Saar problem, and finally in the summer of 1935. I was a frequent visitor to Italy between 1919 and 1926, usually for two or three months at a time. This afforded me ample opportunity to follow the growth of the Fascist movement from its very birth. I was also in Italy in the summer of 1935. My last visits to both Germany and Italy were made with the special purpose of completing the present study. In both countries I discussed the various problems dealt with in the following pages with a large number of people, from high government officials and members of the Fascist and National Socialist parties to their most outspoken opponents. All alike showed me great courtesy and devoted much of their valuable time to answering what must have been to them endless and probably not infrequently tedious questions. For obvious reasons I will refrain from making any specific acknowledgments. I regret this enforced silence because my gratitude is sincere and profound.

Professor Leo Wolman, of Columbia University, was good enough to read the manuscript, and Professor Philip C. Jessup, also of Columbia University, has read my last chapter. They have both made valuable criticisms and suggestions but are, of course, in no way responsible for the opinions I have expressed. I am deeply indebted to Miss A. M., who wishes to remain anonymous, for the translation of the German poem which appears on p. 81. I must also express my very real appreciation of the interest taken in my work by my publishers, The Macmillan Company of New York. The encouragement they have given me has been to no small degree instrumental in the fulfillment of a difficult undertaking. Arthur E. McFarlane has rendered invaluable service to my readers by helping me in my struggles with English. For the imperfections that may still remain my obstinacy alone is to blame. I am also very grateful to Mrs. Cecil P. Killien for her help in preparing this manuscript and for her many useful suggestions.

MICHAEL T. FLORINSKY.

December 9, 1935.
Columbia University, New York City.

CONTENTS

FASCISM

AND

NATIONAL SOCIALISM

CHAPTER I

THE ECLIPSE OF DEMOCRACY: ITALY

THE ROOTS OF FASCISM AND NATIONAL SOCIALISM

In DEALING with such vast national and social movements as Fascism and National Socialism one naturally hesitates to attempt to explain them in terms too simple. Like the Russian Revolution of 1917 these movements have their roots in the past, and cannot be completely understood without an exhaustive study of the political and social conditions in Italy and Germany long before the appearance upon their horizons of Mussolini and Hitler. It became customary among the historians writing on the origins of the war of 1914–1918 to speak of the "immediate" and the "remote" causes of the war. This differentiation will be found useful if applied in the case of Fascism and National Socialism.

Of the remote causes which brought about the downfall of democracy in Italy and Germany little will be said here. The subject is too vast and would require a volume of its own. The immediate causes underlying the appearance of Fascism and National Socialism are also anything but simple. There are one or two, however, that emerge from the cloud of conflicting interpretations and opinions and seem to

1

be of primary importance. The first is the profound disappointment which the outcome of the war brought to both Italy and Germany. Here paradox enters in: a victorious and a defeated nation both found themselves losers at the end of the struggle. Without going into the details of the Italian demands at Versailles and the bitter controversy that raged around the Fiume question and led to the temporary withdrawal of the Italian delegation from the councils of the victorious Powers, it will be enough to recall the fact that Italy obtained no share of the colonial Empire of Germany and had to accept a minor readjustment of the frontier of her African possessions. The expansion in Asia Minor, which was promised her under the terms of the London secret treaty of 1915, failed to materialize. It is true that Rome was given extensive territories in Europe. But these territories were believed by Italy to be less than her due and their economic value proved to be slight. That thirst for imperialistic expansion, which the other Great Powers had satisfied in earlier days and which is behind the venture of Fascism in East Africa, in Italy remained unquenched. The disillusionment of the country found its expression in the well-known Fascist saying that Italy had won the war but lost the peace.

As for Germany, her defeat in 1918 was made even more intolerable by its overwhelming suddenness. To almost the last moment the army and the bulk of the population were still living under the delusion that the hour of victory was merely to be postponed a little longer. After immense sacrifices for what the country believed to be a great national cause Germany's people had to drink to the dregs the bitter cup of humiliation. They had to accept the terms of a treaty which deprived the Fatherland of not only a large portion of its European territory but also of the whole of its colonial empire. Upon Germany there was also imposed what eventually proved to be an intolerable burden of reparations. She was likewise forced to accept the provisions of Article 231 of the Treaty of Versailles which declared her to be the aggressor and which was generally interpreted as meaning that she was responsible for the war. This fateful article played no small part in paving the way for the triumph of National Socialism and in bringing not thousands but millions to rally to the swastika banner. The abyss which separated the glory of the past from the misery of the present was such as few nations have experienced in history.

To this bitter disillusionment and disappointment at the outcome of the war the popular reaction, whether in Italy or in Germany, was the same. Public wrath turned against those who only yesterday had been the great national heroes, and extended to all who took an active part in the war itself. Soldiers in uniform no longer dared appear in the streets for fear of molestation. The doctrines of Socialism and Communism won converts by the thousand, and the red flag began rapidly to displace the national colors. On the horizon loomed what was believed to be the menace of Bolshevik revolution. The "International" was the order of the day, and it was in the nationalist reaction against these conditions that both Fascism and National Socialism found their initial impulse. But the road that led to victory was determined by factors peculiar to each country.

THE BIRTH OF FASCISM

Viewed in retrospect the Italy of 1919–1922 presents an extraordinarily vivid and animated picture, one full of color, excitement and tumult. The sumptuous piazzas of the large cities, with their noble palazzos and majestic cathedrals, and the narrow streets of the small towns and villages were filled with milling and riotous masses of ex-soldiers and men too young to have served in the war, wearing picturesque uniforms and carrying the Italian tricolor, the Fascist insignia, or the red flag of the revolution. The opposing groups often clashed and fought each other with a bitterness and determination which reminded the former soldiers of the most furious and exalted hours of their wartime days. From the aloofness of the Quirinal the Crown watched the rising of new social forces which an impotent Government and an equally impotent Parliament, supported by a complacent, inefficient and corrupt bureaucracy, were unable to check or control. Against the shifting background of ephemeral political combinations often determined by obscure local causes, there outlined itself a no less ephemeral array of political leaders headed by the romantic figure of Gabriel d'Annunzio, poet, soldier and hero of Fiume. But gradually a thunderous voice from Milan and the imperious gesture of Benito Mussolini succeeded in dominating the tumult, and in a few brief months the head of a small band of intellectuals and revolutionaries from the great industrial city of northern Italy rose to undisputed mastery over the country.

The origin of the Fascist movement goes back to the *"Fasci d'Azione Rivoluzionaria"* organized by Mussolini in 1914–1915 for the purpose of bringing Italy into the war, an activity which led to his expulsion from the Socialist Party at the end of November, 1914. There is however no direct connection between these early *fasci* and those which came into existence in 1919, although their spiritual kinship is clear. In either case they were primarily a protest against the inaction, the "neutrality" of the Government, and the political and social system it represented.

The end of the war took Italy, as it took every other country, by surprise. Her economic resources were largely exhausted. Hundreds of thousands of men demobilized from the army were vainly looking for jobs. Inflation led to a rapid increase in prices, continuous demands for higher wages and grave disturbances among industrial workers. Communism was making converts not only among the urban proletariat but also among agricultural laborers. It is one of the peculiarities of the economic structure of Italy that in certain parts of the country agriculture is carried on by the large-scale employment of day laborers. Such districts, for instance, as those around Bologna and Ferrara proved particularly susceptible to extreme Socialist teachings. The unions of rural laborers were largely in the hands of political bosses who, even during the war, practically controlled the entire life of their respective districts, making themselves equally objectionable to landlords and to non-union labor. In certain cities there was also a great deal of discontent among the small traders who felt that they were being crowded out by the aggressive methods of the Socialist cooperative societies. In 1919 and 1920 a number of factories were seized by the workers, some under the national flag, as a protest against the proposed lockouts by the owners, but mostly under the red flag and to the accompaniment of slogans which were more than suggestive of Russian Bolshevism.

Such were the economic factors which underlay the rise of the Fascist movement. It was a struggle against the red revolution, but a struggle conducted not infrequently by groups that were themselves advocating advanced radical doctrines. It was primarily a protest against the inefficiency and weakness of the existing system of government, which had to take the blame for Italy's failure to obtain at Versailles what the country felt it was entitled to. It was also a protest against the violent antimilitarism of the Socialist and Communist groups. They turned their wrath upon the "interventionists" and often insulted and attacked anyone who dared to appear in the streets in uniform. At the best, those who had never seen the firing line treated with contempt men who had spent long months in the trenches and who felt that they had done their duty at the price of immense personal sacrifice; they regarded them as mere puppets in the hands of demagogues who had foolishly forced the Government to espouse the cause of the Allies. Professor Herbert W. Schneider is right when he says in his book, *Making the Fascist State,* that although no doubt the situation which existed in Italy in 1919 was due to economic causes, "the struggle soon assumed a character which no economic interpretation could possibly explain." What Fascism sought to do was to defend and justify the country for having entered the war, to stress the victory it had won, to denounce Bolshevism and the parliamentary system which it held responsible for the paralysis from which the Government was suffering.

Fascism was originally a spontaneous movement, decentralized and uncoordinated. Its aims and its immediate objectives were as varied as the social groups from which it drew its support. Local conditions and the personalities of local leaders had much to do in determining the form of organization and the aims for which it fought. In addition to those mentioned above, some of the *fasci* had definite objectives of their own. The *fasci* of Trieste, for instance, had set themselves against Slavic and those of Bolzano against German influence. While the bulk of the supporters of the Fascist movement came from the lower middle classes and the intellectuals, this was by no means universally true. In Cremona, for example, the movement appealed from the very beginning to the industrial workers, an appeal due in no small degree to the politics of its leader, Farinacci. Some *fasci* had a distinctly intellectual complexion—for instance those of Pisa and Florence. Some were Catholic, others were anticlerical and Free Mason. Some supported the Fiume venture of Gabriel d'Annunzio, others violently opposed it. Some were still upholding the monarchy, while others were strongly republican. Speaking rather loosely, Fascism was a broad social movement which consisted largely of lower middle-class people, intellectuals, students, but also to a lesser extent of workers and, in its later phase, of peasants. It had moreover the support of a number of large industrial and agricultural corporations who saw in it a powerful weapon against Bolshevism. Fascism appealed to the imagination of millions of Italians who cherished the tradition of the *Risorgimento,* the tradition of Garibaldi and Mazzini. It attracted youth in great numbers by its picturesque pageantry, its uniforms, rites, processions and watchwords full of the provocative and reckless spirit of the generation which had known the uplift of victory and the bitterness of defeat. This spirit was accurately if not elegantly expressed in the well-known slogan *"me ne frego,"* or "I don't care a damn." The movement was more-over a kind of haven for those thousands of men who found it so difficult to make a place for themselves in the post-war world.

Following his breach in November 1914 with the Socialist Party, Mussolini devoted all his energies to the cause of "intervention," which to him meant not merely Italy's abandonment of neutrality in the war, but also the starting point of a revolution which was to bring with it real freedom, freedom from the dictatorship "of tiara or sceptre, of sabre or capital, of label or myth." He served with the army, was wounded, and after the war returned with, if possible, even greater fervor than before to his efforts to unite the masses of Italy in their struggle for a better future, even if as yet it was a future that was somewhat vague. The *Popolo d'Italia*, the newspaper he founded in November 1914 after he was forced to resign the editorship of the Socialist *Avanti*, became the organ for his propaganda. Although he was no longer a member of the Socialist Party his paper continued to carry the subtitle, "A Socialist Daily," a subtitle which was accompanied by two maxims: "Revolution is an idea which is based on bayonets" and "Who has steel has bread." It was only after the war that the "Socialist Daily" subtitle was dropped, and replaced by "A daily of fighters and producers." From the end of 1914 to the beginning of 1919 Mussolini was in the peculiar position of a leader with no organization to support him. He had a following, but this following had not

yet gathered itself together and become a definite
political movement.

In Milan on March 23, 1919, Mussolini founded the
Fascio di Combattimento. It had the same objectives as similar groups throughout the country. The
gathering of March 23 was attended by probably not
more than forty-five or fifty men in all, although
larger figures are sometimes given. The new organization had no definite program, except the one "inherent in its name," which meant the defense of
the interests of the "proletariat of the trenches" and,
again, the justifying of intervention. Until the beginning of 1921 the attitude of Mussolini and his
organization was anything but reassuring to the
interests of the property-owning class. With his
struggle against Italian parliamentarism went most
radical demands for economic and social changes.
He advocated the transfer of land to the peasants,
the introduction of the eight-hour day, the participation of the workers in the management of industry,
the nationalization of munition works, a heavy capital levy, a crushing inheritance tax, the confiscation
of 85 per cent of all war profits, and a merciless
shooting of profiteers. This, of course, could hardly
rally the bourgeoisie to his support. The Socialists
never forgave him his "interventionist" attitude of
1914–1915 and his subsequent denunciation of their
policies. The result was that when the Fascists decided to take part in the parliamentary elections of
November 1919, the first elections held under Nitti's
new proportional representation law, they suffered

a crushing defeat, polling merely a few thousand votes. The Socialists won a brilliant victory, and obtained 156 seats. There were many in those days who predicted the complete and final collapse of Fascism. The entire following of Mussolini was estimated at something under 20,000.

He refused, however, to accept defeat. He threw all his indomitable energy into the struggle and events seemed to favor him. In a sense the very success of the Socialists worked against them, for it aroused the fears of the proprietor groups and the middle class. It was with much apprehension that they contemplated the possibility of a Government that might be a duplicate of Russian Bolshevism. At the same time Socialist municipalities and institutions of local government frequently practised petty tyrannies of the most vexatious kind. The unions of agricultural workers were more aggressive than ever. In August and September 1920 a number of large industrial plants in the north of Italy were seized by the workers, and although the matter was in time settled peacefully, as a result of negotiations on the part of the Giolitti Government, fears of a repetition of such things remained. Indeed, the Government itself was suspected by many to be too much under the influence of radical elements. As for Mussolini and his Fascists the fact that they were fighting the Socialists, who were in a majority in Parliament and controlled much of the country's administrative machinery, made many feel that *his* radicalism, after all, was not perhaps quite so dan-

gerous as on the surface it might seem to be. His
followers, gathering new recruits, fought under
patriotic banners. Their slogan was "Down with the
red menace!" And they made their campaign
against the Socialists a bitter one. In 1920–1922
Italy was in a condition that closely resembled civil
war. In various parts of the country open conflicts
between Fascists and Socialists occurred almost
daily, and were often accompanied by much blood-
shed and destruction of property. The Fascists went
to the length of destroying or burning down Socialist
clubs, newspaper offices, cooperative society headquarters and the like. Both police and Government
maintained an almost hands-off attitude, which on
more than one occasion seemed to favor the assail-
ants. Eventually Giolitti, whose policy was one of
expediency and the desire to remain in office, openly
turned against his former Socialist allies and began
actively to support the Fascists. In March 1921 he
dissolved Parliament and there was a new election.
In this, too, Mussolini's program was largely directed against Bolshevism and proclaimed the necessity of saving the country from the horrors of class
war—as preached by the Socialists. The radical
economic and social demands of his 1919 platform
were kept much in the background. The Fascists
also entered into a *bloc* with the Nationalists. It
was successful. They won thirty-four seats while the
Socialists lost the same number. Mussolini and his
followers took their seats on the extreme right, and
in his speech as leader of the group he declared that

he was "reactionary because he was anti-parliamentarian, anti-democratic and anti-socialist."

THE FASCIST PARTY

It was an important victory for Fascism and it was followed by far-reaching changes in organization. Until the end of 1921 it had been a movement, not a party. This was considered by many of its leaders, including Dino Grandi and Italo Balbo, who is today Air Marshal of Italy and Governor of Libya, to be one of the essential conditions of success. Mussolini himself had earlier forcibly advanced the same view. The absence of any definite party name or party program was the living symbol of the sort of freedom, ultimate but not yet clearly seen, that he had so often extolled. And it had been feared that the formalization of the movement into a party might alienate many of its followers or even bring about its complete collapse. Nevertheless at a Congress in Rome on November 7, 1921, the foundation of a definite Fascist Party was decided upon. There were various reasons for this decision. A parliamentary group without a party behind it was an obvious anomaly. The local *fasci* were too much under the influence of their immediate leaders and could not always be counted upon for support. The transforming of the movement into a party would be a first step toward the creation of that reliable machine which was now considered essential if the future of Fascism was to be assured. Mussolini, it would seem, was also somewhat alarmed by the number and brutality of the acts of violence committed by his supporters, though it was violence that he himself had preached and encouraged. In August 1921 he even entered into an agreement with the Socialists and the Confederation of Labor designed to prevent future outbursts. This agreement was bitterly criticized within the Fascist Party, nearly wrecked it, and led Mussolini to offer his resignation. But it was not accepted and later the agreement was denounced by the Fascists. As for the organized party, however, it was clearly a more efficient instrument for keeping its members under control than was the loose and informal discipline which formerly prevailed among the scattered Fascist groups.

At the Rome Congress the party program was duly accepted. In the traditional and involved Fascist phraseology it spoke of the Nation and the State, denounced Socialism, praised labor, and declared itself in favor of economic liberalism on the ground that the economic activities of a nation must not be handed over to the control of bureaucratic agencies. This certainly could not displease business, large or small, sorely tried as it had been by several years of Socialist experimentation.

The Congress of Rome was attended by representatives of 2,200 *fasci*, groups that together numbered a total of some 310,000 members. This was a considerable increase over the twenty *fasci* with 17,000 members that were represented in 1919 at the Fascist Congress in Florence. But it was still merely a fraction of Italy's 43 millions. Not that the relative insignificance of the number of his followers was anything in itself to disturb Mussolini. The principle of hierarchy and leadership by an *élite* that would embody the highest aspirations of the Nation formed one of the fundamental ideas of Fascism. The important thing was to make this *élite* strong enough to impose its will upon the masses. The Party therefore proceeded to reorganize the *fasci* into more coherent elements, into formations that were almost military and indeed much on the pattern of the Roman legions. Furthermore they now accepted the strictest discipline and gave their complete allegiance to the Party and the Duce. In a proclamation issued on November 21, 1921, the Party was literally described as a "voluntary militia placed at the service of the State," a definition which was retained with some variations in the subsequent constitutions of the Party. The State it was prepared to serve, however, was not the parliamentary régime of the Pre-Fascist era. Bonomi, the new head of the Government, was under no illusions about that and he ordered the prefects both to take arms from those in possession of them, and to cancel all permits. But this order was never put into effect for the local authorities themselves were too deeply entangled in the Fascist movement.

The next step in the consolidation of the Fascist advance to power was an attempt to capture the very stronghold of Socialism, the trade-union move-

ment. In 1921 Fascist trade unions began to spring
up all over the country. They obtained a considerable degree of success, especially among the poorer
elements of the working people who frequently had
to endure harsh treatment at the hands of their local
labor bosses.

THE MARCH ON ROME

The year 1922 saw the final stages of the collapse
of the democratic régime and the steady taking over
of the government, in the provinces, by the Fascist
leaders. The absence of any parliamentary majority
made the functioning of the representative government pure illusion. One political crisis followed another in an almost endless succession. They were
finally resolved into mere shiftings of ministerial
portfolios within the same small clique of professional politicians. Central authority was made nil.
Outside Rome the pressure of the Fascist organizations became greater day by day. Town after town
and commune after commune passed under their
control. In August 1922 they completely suppressed
the Socialists in Milan and destroyed the plant of
Avanti, the paper which had once had Mussolini for
its editor. At almost the same time Genoa, once the
stronghold of Socialism, was occupied by Fascist
forces, and *Il Lavoro,* another important Socialist
publication, perished in the flames. A general strike
which the Socialists had begun earlier in the summer and which was the immediate cause of the

Fascist invasion of Milan and Genoa collapsed miserably.

The situation was rapidly becoming intolerable. It was obvious that the Rome Government was being superseded by Fascism as the *de facto* ruler of the country. It was merely a question of by what methods Fascism was to reach power. Some of its leaders favored legality and a peaceful penetration into the machinery of government. But others called for open insurrection, for the "March on Rome." This was something that had been in the air ever since d'Annunzio had made his spectacular entry into Fiume, and it made a strong appeal to the more exuberant element in the Party. Finally, too, pressure in favor of this means of bringing matters to a solution became irresistible, even though, as a consequence of the complete surrender of the Government and of the King, the culmination of the "March" proved to be a rather mild affair.

The March on Rome was decided upon at the end of September 1922. On October 18 a special Quadrumvirate was named to mobilize the forces of Fascism for the great event. On October 24 some 50,000 black shirts gathered in Naples for a Party congress. Mussolini, so long an ardent republican, had now changed his attitude toward the throne. "I do not think," he declared, "that the monarchy has really any object in opposing what must now be called 'the Fascist revolution.' . . . The monarchy represents the historical continuity of the Nation; a splendid function, and one of incalculable importance." This and similar statements were, no doubt, of great importance in shaping the events that followed. On October 28 the March on Rome began. A proclamation issued by the Fascists announced that it was not to be directed against the King, the army or the "productive elements" of the country, but solely against those who had betrayed it. As Mussolini put it, in his speech at Naples, "The Chamber no longer represents the country, and every minister exercises his powers illegally. Our duty is to restore legality to the representative institutions of Italy."

Luigi Facta, who headed the shadowy government then in office, decided to oppose the advance of the Fascists. A state of siege was declared but the order had to be countermanded for the King refused to sign the decree. While the black-shirted cohorts were closing in on Rome Mussolini was offered the opportunity to become part of a coalition government, but declined. On the 29th the King called him to Rome, and the next day, amid scenes of extraordinary enthusiasm, he formed a government. Then, on the 31st, he issued an order for the demobilization of his black shirts. Officially, but only officially, the revolution was over. Actually Italy was opening a new page in her history.

MUSSOLINI AND PARLIAMENT

"Democracy has destroyed the essential nature of the Italian people," said Mussolini shortly before the March on Rome, "that is, not only the character but the color, the force, the picturesque, the unexpected, the mystic, all in fact that lies deep in the soul of our people. But we shall restore it all. We shall play on every string from violence to religion, from art to politics. We are statesmen and we are warriors." Yet the steps by which he proceeded to give reality to this vague program—if it can be called a program—were such as not many of his followers expected.

In spite of his avowed aversion to parliamentarianism he began his official career as head of a coalition government. His first cabinet was largely drawn from political groups not belonging to the Fascist Party. He appeared before the two Houses of Parliament, showed much deference to the Senate but gave rough handling to the Chamber of Deputies. However it accepted the scolding resignedly and obediently voted the measures that the Government demanded. The Duce had made it clear that they would be put into effect in any case. The main efforts of the new régime were now, and for the first two or three years of its existence, devoted to consolidating its position. This demanded, on the one hand, the strengthening of the machinery of the Party and, on the other, the removal from all offices, however humble, of every enemy of Fascism.

The membership of the Party was subjected to a close scrutiny and was drastically purged of undesirable elements. To determine what were the unde-

sirable elements proved by no means an easy business. It was a difficulty for which, in no small degree,
the uncertainties in the Fascist doctrine were themselves responsible. But ever since these periodical
purges have continued to be one of the characteris-
tics of Fascism. No less significant was the dissolution of all individual Fascist fighting units by an
order of the Grand Council of Fascism, issued January 12, 1923. They were replaced by the Fascist
Militia; and in July of the same year this Militia
received its constitution. The Militia consisted of
picked men and its chief business was declared to be
the defense of the régime and the preservation of
public order. Organized on military lines, bound together by a strict discipline, sworn to absolute obedience, and imbued with boundless and fanatical devotion to the Duce this Militia has to this day been
one of the mainstays of Fascist rule.

It played no small part indeed in the accomplishing of Fascism's second task, the reconstruction of
the administrative machinery of the country and the
removal from office of all those whose attachment to
the new leader might be questioned. Various methods of pressure were used to make former office-
holders give place to men who were favored by the
local Fascist powers. In a number of cases the
municipal councils and other institutions of local
government were merely put aside and replaced by
commissioners appointed by royal decrees or by orders of the prefects. This process offered practically
unbounded opportunities for abuses of the grossest

nature, and for the strengthening of the local Fascist bosses, on whom the Government and the Party found it necessary to put a check in the reforms of 1925–1928.

In the meantime Mussolini continued to play the rather unexpected part of a constitutional prime minister, one, too, who had no assured majority in Parliament. In November 1922 wide emergency powers were granted to him by the legislature. The first important change in the constitution came with the Election Law of July 1923. It was duly voted by the Chamber when Mussolini plainly warned it that the fate of the parliamentary régime was in the balance. This law provided that the political party which obtained the largest number of electoral votes should receive two-thirds of the seats, provided that it polled not less than 25 per cent of the total vote. The elections took place on April 6, 1924. A year earlier, in March 1923, the Nationalists had been absorbed in the Fascist Party and their candidates appeared in the same National or Fascist lists. Mussolini issued definite orders to insure the fairness of the elections, but it is generally admitted that these orders were not really enforced. The Militia was mobilized on election day and intimidation and corrupt practices were widely resorted to. The Fascist list received 4.8 million votes. Next to them came the Socialists, but they had only one million. The other parties received considerably less. Mussolini, with 268 seats in the possession of his supporters might well have seemed to be in a position to carry through all the reforms he desired. Unexpectedly, however, the minority parties proved recalcitrant. When the new Parliament assembled, the opposition with vigor and vehemence assailed the Government's conduct of the elections and its policies in general. Montecitorio again became the scene of violent recriminations which were reminiscent of pre-Fascist days. Prominent among the denouncers of Fascism was the Socialist deputy, Matteotti. On June 10, 1924, he was murdered and a number of high Fascist dignitaries, belonging to the immediate *entourage* of Mussolini, were involved in the sinister affair. The murder and the revelations which followed produced a tremendous sensation. There was general clamor from the opposition for the disbanding of the Militia, the restoration of proportional representation and new elections. In the end the opposition even refused to continue to sit in the Chamber and left Montecitorio altogether. This won them the sobriquet of the "Aventino" Opposition, as was only natural in a country where classical traditions are still alive. Mussolini made several attempts at conciliation, but failed. A new wave of unrest was sweeping the country, with wild outbursts from both sides. At the end of 1924, exasperated by personal attacks, he saw that all hopes of reconciliation were out of the question. He declared open war on the "Aventino" and all other enemies of the régime. His official excuse for the drastic measures which followed was the same excuse he had used so often in the past, "the red menace." The Chamber of Deputies, minus the opposition, continued to function and passed the bills introduced by the Government. When some of the "Aventino" members attempted to resume their seats they were not permitted to do so, and finally their mandates were declared annulled.

TOWARD A DICTATORSHIP

A rapid succession of measures made a clean sweep of the civic liberties the Italians had enjoyed in the past. Freedom of the press, of speech, of meeting and assembly, was gone. Under the new laws any expression of opinion unfavorable to Fascism could be construed as a serious offense, subject to heavy penalties. Special courts were established to deal with offenses of this kind, and such courts were kept very busy. The entire machinery of the judiciary was put under the supervision of the executive and lost its former independence. The powerful Masonic lodges were closed. Political parties other than the Fascist disappeared. The totalitarian State was distinctly in the making.

Far-reaching changes also took place in the local and central administration. The powers of the prefect were much extended. Elected mayors were replaced by *Podestà* appointed by the Ministry of the Interior. These measures were directed not only against the enemies of Fascism but also against those local Fascist bosses who frequently had paid small heed to the wishes of the central government and the Party leaders. The elective provincial and municipal councils were abolished and replaced by advisory committees appointed by local interests under the supervision of the Party. Local autonomy, largely fictitious even in pre-Fascist days, was now replaced by a rigid centralization.

The central government of the Kingdom suffered an even greater root and branch readjustment. By a law of December 24, 1924, the office of *Capo del Governo* or Head of the Government was established. Appointed by the King, the Head of the Government was given unlimited power to determine the destinies of the country. The members of his cabinet occupied a very subordinate position. The Head of the Government was to "direct and coordinate" their work and settle any differences which may arise among them. It became, moreover, the Fascist practice to have from time to time a "changing of the guard," when all or almost all the members of the cabinet would tender their resignations and be replaced by new men, for no special purpose except that of injecting new blood into the administrative body.

Parliament, after its unexpected revolt that had precipitated the political crisis of 1924–1925, was naturally among the institutions which were to be completely remodelled. After much discussion the new law here called for was drafted by the Grand Council and, in 1928, obediently passed by the Chamber of Deputies. Under this legislation the Chamber now consists of four hundred members elected by the Grand Council of Fascism from one thousand names submitted to it by the confederations of employers and employees, of which more will be said later, and by a number of other organizations. The Council has the right to add other "distinguished" names to the list, which is then submitted to the electors. If the list obtains 50 per cent of the vote all those whose names are upon it are elected. There are provisions for the preparation of lists other than that of the Grand Council but these provisions are of purely academic interest. The confederations and other associations which submit names to the Grand Council for inclusion in the list of future deputies are all controlled by the Fascist Party. Under these conditions the character of the Chamber is a foregone conclusion. Officially, elections are perfectly free and secret, but there seems to be much local pressure, and apprehension on the part of the voters that secrecy is not quite so complete as might be desired. At the election of 1929 8.5 million voted "Yes" under the Fascist list and 135,000 "No." In 1934 10 million voted "Yes" and only 15,000 "No." Great efforts have been made to triumph over the apathy of the electors, which is not difficult to understand with an electoral system like the one described above. This "parliament" can hardly be regarded as any genuine expression of the opinion of the country. But it serves the useful purpose of performing a certain amount of technical legislative work and also of keeping the Duce in direct contact if not with the opinion of the country at least with the opinion of the broader Fascist circles.

Mussolini has little liking for the legislative assembly which he himself installed at Montecitorio. Since the creation of "corporations," which will be dealt with in a subsequent chapter, there has been much discussion of the necessity of abolishing the Chamber of Deputies altogether. "Running ahead of time some have already spoken of the end of the present Chamber of Deputies," said Mussolini on November 14, 1933. ". . . The time will come when the Chamber of Deputies will have to decide its own fate. Are there any Fascists who feel inclined to weep at this possibility? If there are, let them know that we shall not dry their tears. It is quite conceivable that the National Council of Corporations will wholly replace the present Chamber. It has never been a thing that I liked. Its very name has become an anachronism. It is an institution which we inherited, and which is alien to our mentality and to our Fascist passion. The Chamber presupposes that a world which we have demolished is still alive. It presupposes the plurality of parties and would mean frequent attacks upon the ministerial coach. Since the day on which we annulled this plurality the Chamber has lacked the fundamental reason for which it was established. . . . But all these are developments for the future, and there is no undue haste." There can be no doubt therefore as to the real intentions of the Duce with reference to the Chamber of Deputies. In the meantime it swells the

list of places distributed by the Government and
the Party to their deserving followers.

THE PARTY AND THE STATE

The most striking constitutional innovation of the
Fascist régime is the establishment of the Grand
Council of Fascism as the central institution of the
government. The Grand Council entered upon its
career in January 1923 and was then merely a committee of the leaders of the Fascist Party. In those
days it concerned itself with Party policies and had
no direct connection with affairs of state, although
its powers were continuously expanding with the
growth of the influence of the Party on the administration of public business. It was the Grand Council that appointed the Commission on the Constitution which made the proposal for the legislative
changes briefly discussed above. In 1926 the Fascist
Party received its first formal constitution, and
thereafter it became necessary to formalize its relations with the constitutional machinery already in
existence. By the Law of December 9, 1928,
amended by the Law of December 14, 1929, the
Grand Council of Fascism was accordingly made the
central organ of the constitution of the State. It is,
of course, like all other important institutions of the
régime, under the complete and unlimited control
of the Head of the Government. He is the Council's
chairman. The membership of the Council consists
of the higher officials of the Party and of the State,

such as members of the cabinet, the presidents of
the Senate and the Chamber of Deputies, and also
members appointed by the Head of the Government.

The functions of the Grand Council are of the utmost importance. It must be consulted on all constitutional changes in contemplation—and the Law
offers an exhaustive list of them. They cover changes
in the order of succession to the throne. The Council also keeps a list of names of persons proposed by
the Head of the Government, which list is to be submitted to the King to guide him in appointing a successor to the Duce in case his office should become
vacant; and it likewise keeps similar lists of candidates for other high offices, which are to be sent to
the King in case of an emergency, though the normal exercise of this function is one of the preroga-
tives of the Head of the Government. The Grand
Council is linked with all the central institutions of
the State and of the Party. It controls them all and
is the living symbol of that totalitarian idea of the
Fascist State which makes the Party the dominating
element in the life of the State. The constitution of
the Fascist Party is subject to Royal approval on
the recommendation of the Head of the Government. The Secretary of the Party is appointed by
the King at the request of the Duce. The Commission of the Chamber which reported on the Law was
perfectly justified therefore in stating that "the
Party . . . becomes completely an organ of the
State." In accordance with the language of its Sta-

tutes the Fascist Party is a "civil Militia, at the orders of the Duce, at the service of the Fascist State." The State and the Party are thus inextricably bound together, and the Duce who heads both is supreme.

Nominally the Crown is still the highest authority. But the King is hardly more than a prisoner in the Quirinal. Any independent political action on his part is entirely outside the realm of possibility. As a tangible embodiment of Italy's historical tradition he is a useful attribute and one that enhances the prestige of the Fascist régime. The Crown was led to accept its present position by the events that followed the fateful decision of the King on October 29. It is possible, too, that the acceptance of the inevitable was made more palatable not only by those marks of external respect which are forthcoming today from quarters where, before 1922, they were altogether lacking, but also by the realization that if it were not for the Fascist régime the monarchy in Italy might well by now be a thing of the past.

CHAPTER II

THE ECLIPSE OF DEMOCRACY: GERMANY

THE SETTING

THE Germany that gave birth to the National Socialist movement was no less racked and harassed than the Italy of 1919–1922. Indeed its position was even grimmer. No political régime ever began under worse auguries than the ill-fated Weimar Republic. Looking back at the recent history of Germany one feels that even under the most favorable conditions the chances of a democratic form of government taking firm root in the soil of the former German Empire would not have been too bright. Prussia's long domination over the Reich had left upon it an imprint that neither the defeat of 1918 nor the thirteen years of republican administration that followed were able to efface. The institutions of democracy, like any other human institutions, cannot be transplanted forcibly into a soil that is alien and in which all the elements needed for their growth and development are wholly lacking. The new-born German Republic, moreover, had to assume from its very first steps an utterly intolerable burden. A government consisting of men with little or no experience in public office was confronted with problems which would have taxed to the very limit the ingenuity of the shrewdest statesmen. In 1918–1919 the country was in the depths of despair. Military defeat, it will be remembered, descended upon Germany as crushingly as it was unexpected. For over four years the army and the civilian population had endured almost superhuman hardships in a struggle for what they believed to be a just cause. Cut off from the rest of the world by the iron ring of the naval blockade, Germany had been reduced to depend solely on the resources of herself and those of her three Allies; and they largely depended on her for military and technical equipment. She had put all her organizing genius and all her capacity to resist into the service of the great national cause, that of winning the war. And then had come the complete collapse. It was really more than a military defeat. It was the crumbling of an entire world, the destruction of traditional spiritual values which left behind them a vacuum that has perhaps not yet been filled. All the sacrifices of the past had proved to be in vain. The present was bleak, the future so forbidding that one hardly dared face it.

The spiritual crisis that Germany lived through, then, had a fitting counterpart in her complete economic prostration. The accumulated wealth of the country had gone to the financing of the war. Gone were some of her most important industrial regions such as Alsace-Lorraine, the Saar, and parts of Upper Silesia. Old industrial ties had been ruthlessly severed. Both agriculture and industry were disorganized and found it difficult to adjust themselves to the new world which emerged from the war. Tariff barriers and trade restrictions were rising menacingly in every part of Central Europe and made necessary the drastic revision of the old-established trade routes. The depreciation of the mark was the forerunner of inflation which was to reach its zenith in 1923. It brought in its wake the financial collapse of Germany's middle class, the ruin of people with fixed incomes, and offered at the same time almost unlimited opportunities for the accumulation of large fortunes by unscrupulous speculators. These *nouveaux riches* complacently and ostentatiously displayed their wealth, and this made keener the misery of their fellow citizens who had lost their modest all in the catastrophe that had overtaken the Nation. Seldom can contrasts between poverty and wealth have been greater. Seldom can the population of an advanced industrial country have been reduced to such misery. Hundreds of thousands of men demobilized from the army were returning with hearts heavy with bitterness to their chill and darkened homes, with little hope of finding work and making a living.

The ground for the spreading of the most radical doctrine was all prepared. Across the eastern frontier, over the head of Poland, came the passionate appeals of Lenin, Trotsky and Zinoviev who called for the immediate establishment of the dictatorship of the proletariat. And those were days when the thing appeared to be by no means impossible. The *Spartakus* uprising took place in Berlin

in 1919 and was followed by similar bloody outbursts in other parts of the country. Hungary was
already under the rule of Bela Kun, and a Soviet
resolution had flared up in Munich. Men and
women who had lost all faith in an existing order
that had brought to them such untold misery were
rapidly swelling the membership of the Communist
Party.

The worst thing, however, that had been laid
upon the new German Republican Government was
the compulsion it was under to put its signature to
the Treaty of Versailles. The result was that almost
from the first *Das System,* as the Weimar Republic
was soon to be called by her opponents, was tainted
with the disgrace of having accepted the hated *Diktat* which saddled Germany with the responsibility
for the war and compelled her to force its penalties
upon an unwilling German people. The truly remarkable thing about the Versailles Treaty is not its
failure to embody the highest principles of equity,
but the fact that any agreement at all could have
been reached by the victorious Powers in the atmosphere of unreality and fantastic delusions that prevailed in 1919.[1] The provisions of the Treaty that
proved particularly poisonous from the point of view
of international relations were those which, in their
very nature, prevented the German wounds from
healing. Such were the articles that called for the
occupation of the western side of the Rhine by Allied

---

[1] At the Versailles Conference, for instance, Germany's *capacity
to pay* was estimated by one learned British "expert" at 480 billion gold marks, and by a French "expert" at 800 billion!

troops for fifteen years, the demilitarization of the left bank of the Rhine (a provision which is still in effect and is bound, sooner or later, to become the source of international complications), the limitation of German armament repudiated by Hitler in March 1935, and, above all, the reparation payments. The latter question was left open by the Treaty and was to be settled by the Reparation Commission. This led to endless and most vexatious negotiations between the Allies and Germany— negotiations which brought with them the occupation of the Ruhr by the French and Belgians in 1923—and a number of shadowy settlement schemes all of which, with the exception of the Dawes Plan,[2] ended in failure. The acceptance of each of these schemes by the Reich was accompanied by much international bitterness, by much pressure upon Germany on the part of the Allies and by new waves of indignation and criticism in Germany herself; and such feelings vented themselves not only against the former enemy Powers but also against the home government, because it had been unable to save the country from "economic slavery." The policy of "fulfillment" of the Treaty was one of the chief arguments used against the *System* by its opponents. The administration of reparations and other provisions of the Treaty, moreover, necessitated the establishment at different times of agencies of Allied

[2] The privileged position of the Dawes Plan was due merely to the fact that it was "provisional"; it was duly replaced in 1929 by the Young Plan, which was described as the "final settlement." It collapsed a year later.

control for the supervision of the economic life of Germany. The activities and the very presence on German soil of such bodies was naturally much resented. The cumulative effect of the Allied policy toward Germany following the war was to weaken the position of Germany's new and democratic Government by making it, in the opinion of many Germans, a reluctant, but nevertheless obedient, tool for the achievement of Allied aims. This was certainly a vital factor in stimulating the growth of that aggressive and militant nationalism which is the backbone of the Hitler movement.

It is true that the Allies from time to time made important concessions. Some of the provisions of the Treaty were never enforced and were permitted to lapse. The western side of the Rhine was evacuated in 1930, five years before the expiration of the prescribed time. Reparations themselves were written off for all practical purposes at Lausanne in 1932, although legally they could still be revived. Germany however refused to look upon these concessions as friendly gestures or the abandonment of rightful claims, for she had never accepted the Versailles Treaty as a just and equitable peace. The Republican Government therefore got little or no credit for what it might well consider to be substantial diplomatic victories. As time went on, instead of gaining ground it grew steadily weaker.

This weakness, of course, was by no means entirely due to the policy of the Allies. There was a sharp cleavage between the German Social Democratic Party and the German Communist Party. The latter was entirely under the dominance of the Third International which, in those days, considered the Social Democrats as among its worse enemies. Looking for support, the German Social Democrats retained the officer corps of the former imperial army as an organizing cadre for the *Reichswehr*. They also retained the old judiciary and much of the former civil service, including the diplomatic corps. None of these elements had ever been completely reconciled to the Republic, and they were certainly not hostile to the possibility of a change in the form of government. The Social Democrats did practically nothing to break the power of the industrial magnates and the landed aristocracy. Article 155 (ii) of the Weimar Constitution which envisaged the possibility of expropriation of land for the needs of internal colonization was never put into practice. On the contrary, owners of large estates were generously supported by the Republican Government which bestowed large subsidies on them. All things considered, in spite of the fall of the monarchy and the growth of Communism, the social structure of Germany under the Weimar Republic was not substantially different from what it was before the Revolution. It must also be admitted that the democratic system never worked satisfactorily. Between February 1919 and January 1933 Germany had 21 cabinets headed by 12 chancellors. Not less than 38 parties participated in the elections to the Reichstag in 1932.

THE HITLER MOVEMENT

To understand the rise of the Hitler movement it is important to keep this political and economic background in mind. As for its beginnings they were even more humble than those of Italian Fascism. As we have seen, even before the war Mussolini was a leader with a national reputation, and the *fasci* had spontaneously organized all over the country. Adolf Hitler was, in 1919, a man entirely unknown, an Austrian German who had first come to Germany in 1912. During the war he fought in the German army. He had been wounded and gassed, and had won the Iron Cross. Until 1920 he had continued to serve in the army, holding the rank of corporal (*Gefreite*). He had no following of any kind. In 1919 he was invited to a meeting of the German Workers Party (*Deutsche Arbeiterpartei*) which had been founded in January of the same year by a locksmith, Anton Drexler. The party was not really a party at all, but merely a small group of men united by their refusal to accept the "betrayal" of the army which they felt had been "stabbed in the back." It was a group which at that time numbered twenty-eight members. But only six of them were active, and when Hitler joined the organization in July 1919 he received membership card No. 7. A little later the German Workers Party added to its name and became the National Socialist German Workers Party (*Nationalsozialistische Deutsche Arbeiterpartei*). On August 1, 1921, Hitler was elected its

leader. A year before, on February 24, 1920, the
Party had adopted an official program which had
been drafted by Gottfried Feder, an engineer, the
effect of whose writings on Hitler's own outlook he
gratefully acknowledges in *Mein Kampf*. This program, which was expounded in twenty-five para-
graphs, was clothed in language rather ambiguous
and obscure. It contained some very radical demands, such as the abolition of all unearned incomes
and the "slavery of interest" (*Brechung der Zins-
knechtschaft*), the confiscation of war profits, the nationalization of trusts, profit-sharing in large concerns, an expansion of the old-age pension system,
public ownership of department stores, the expropriation of land for public purposes, the elimination
of land rent, the prevention of land speculation, and
free primary education. The program, moreover, demanded the cancellation of the Treaty of Versailles,
and developed the idea of "Germany for the Germans" by calling for a policy of treating as for-
eigners all those who were not of German blood. "No
Jews therefore can be members of the Nation." All
such persons were to be deprived of the right to hold
any public office, own newspapers or engage in jour-
nalistic work. All non-Germans who had entered the
country since August 2, 1914, were to be deported.
The program also proclaimed the principle of "the
interests of all before the interests of one" (*Gemeinnutz vor Eigennutz*) and advocated a strong central
government with absolute authority over the entire
Reich and all its organizations. The preamble to the

program said that this was a "time program" (*Zeit-Program*). By a decision of the Party on May 22, 1926, it was nevertheless declared to be "unchangeable," which, however, was officially stated to mean that "the fundamental principles and the fundamental ideas of this program cannot be altered," but that the methods by which it was to be carried out were to be adapted to changing conditions. That some of the most fundamental principles of National Socialism were open to more than one interpretation appears from the important official statement issued by Hitler on April 13, 1928. Here he pointed out that the Party bases its policy on the right of private property, and that the expression "expropriation of land without compensation" applied only to land unlawfully acquired or not used in the public interest. "It is therefore primarily directed against Jewish speculators in land." This elucidation of the real meaning of "expropriation of land without compensation" undoubtedly went a long way toward reconciling landed proprietors to National Socialism.

The following of the National Socialist Party in its early days was largely drawn from various private military organizations (*Freikorps*) which were numerous in Germany after the war. Captain Ernest Röhm, who lost his life in the bloody "purge" of June 30, 1934, was among the army officers who joined the Party in 1919 and was largely instrumental in recruiting men for the S. A. (*Sturm Abteilung*) which became the counterpart of the Fascist Militia. What attracted these young men to National Socialism was not so much its official program as its militant spirit, its hatred of the Versailles Treaty and of anyone associated with it, its quasi-military organization, and the opportunities to fight those whom they believed to be the enemies of "true Germany." These were in particular the "Marxist-Liberal State," the Communists and the Jews. For anti-Semitism has been from the very beginning one of the outstanding features of the Hitler movement.

Although National Socialism was increasing its membership, the increase in the early years was not spectacular. Only six thousand S. A. men were present at the first Party Congress (*Parteitag*) in January 1923. In November 1923 Hitler participated, with General Ludendorff, in the abortive *Putsch* in Munich, the failure of which is ascribed by the National Socialist commentators to the betrayal by one of the leaders of the uprising, von Kahr. Hitler was arrested, tried and sentenced to five years in prison. It was during his confinement in Landsberg that he wrote *Mein Kampf*. Many of Hitler's lieutenants were also behind the bars. The Party was virtually outlawed. It might well have seemed that National Socialism had been wiped out of existence.

THE RISING TIDE

But this was not the case. On March 4, 1924, the remnants of the Party, in a *bloc* with the German

People's Party (*Deutschvölkische Partei*) participated in the Reichstag elections and obtained thirty-two seats. At the time the trial of Hitler was taking place and as it was being given much publicity this probably had something to do with the *bloc's* comparative success. On December 20, 1924, Hitler was released and he immediately proceeded to reorganize the Party. In February 1925 the *Völkische Beobachter*, the Party organ, the publication of which had been suspended since the Munich affair, again began to appear, and the remaining members of the movement, so lately scattered, reassembled under the swastika banner and reaffirmed their confidence in their leader. In the years that followed, the growth of the movement was slow. In the Reichstag elections of May 20, 1928, the National Socialists obtained only 800,000 votes, but they won twelve seats, an increase of eight over what they had held before. Their former ally, the German People's Party, was practically wiped out of existence. In 1929 the National Socialist Party combined with the German Nationalist Party (*Deutschnationale Volkspartei*) in an attempt to block the adoption of the Young Plan. They succeeded in forcing a referendum but only 5.8 million ballots were cast. The major parties refrained from voting, and the proposed rejection of the Young Plan was defeated. It was, however, National Socialism's last important setback. The tide was turning in its favor with a rapidity which the earlier slowness of its rise did not seem to forecast.

In the Reichstag election of September 1930 the
Hitler movement obtained 6.5 million votes and 107
seats. There was great elation among the members
and open talk of a "March on Berlin." In the presidential elections in the spring of 1932 Hitler was
defeated by von Hindenburg but obtained 11.3 million votes on the first ballot and 13.4 million votes
on the second. From the election of July 1932 the
National Socialists emerged as the strongest party in
the Reichstag. They had won 230 seats and polled
a total vote of 13.7 millions. The Social Democrats
trailed far behind with 133 seats. The dissolution of
the Reichstag by von Papen was followed in November by a new election which registered a setback
for National Socialism. The movement got 11.7 million votes and only 196 seats, while the representation of the Communists was somewhat increased.
There was much speculation as to the "inevitable"
decline of the Hitler movement, although the rapid
winning over of the institutions of local government
by the National Socialists and their increasing
strength in the legislatures of the various States
gave little ground for such conjectures. Within the
movement there was some criticism of the leader's
tactics. In October 1931 Hitler and Göring were
consulted by Hindenburg, but nothing came of it.
Hitler was again called in by Hindenburg in November 1932, but refused to participate in a coalition
government which he was not to head. It was generally believed that he had missed his chance and
that a movement which preached direct action but

in practice limited itself to street-corner fisticuffs with the Communists was bound to disintegrate. But on January 30 Hindenburg once more called Hitler in and this time the Führer emerged from the presidential palace as Chancellor of the German Reich and head of a coalition government composed of National Socialists, Nationalists and conservative-minded men, some of whom had served in the von Papen and von Schleicher cabinets.

The sudden turn in the fortunes of National Socialism between 1928 and 1930, when its Reichstag vote increased from 800,000 to 6.5 millions and its almost uninterrupted progress thereafter calls for closer study. National Socialist writers, I think, rightly emphasize the parallel between the growth of the Party and the growth of unemployment. In the large cities 60 or 70 per cent of the membership of the S. A. is said to have consisted of the unemployed. So long as economic conditions were improving and recovery was being stimulated by a generous current of gold which, in the form of loans, continued to turn the wheels of industry faster and faster, the Hitler movement made little headway. But the collapse of the mechanism for international loans and the decline in international trade, to say nothing of all the other concomitants of depression, brought in their wake a most rapid increase in the number of unemployed who, by January 1933, numbered more than six million. The deflationary policies of Brüning contributed to the increase of the national burden, and their effects were particularly felt by the lower middle class among whom Hitler found the main body of his supporters.

We must also remember that National Socialism had always claimed to be a movement of the young; and, by 1930, the children of the war years had grown to manhood. They had grown up, too, at a time when the country, as we have seen, was passing through a period of extremely painful readjustment. They had lived through many hardships. They could see no justice in international financial arrangements, such as the Young Plan, that were to lay upon their country a heavy financial burden that was to last for three generations, as a penalty for a war in which these generations had had no part. They were losing faith in a social and economic system that resulted in poverty in the midst of plenty, and they were not resigned to accepting without a struggle a future that had nothing in store for them except unemployment. The militant character of the Hitler movement, its thrills and novelty, its uniforms, fist fights with the police and Communists, and all of its heroic trappings and phraseology appealed irresistibly to the romantic element in the German character. From the drab world of daily drudgery and waiting lines at the doors of employment offices, National Socialism was taking its youthful followers to that exalted realm where sacrifice for a great national cause was ardently preached in a language which, if perhaps not always clear or logical, succeeded in touching some deep inner chords of the human heart. The mixture of brutality, racial pride, anti-Semitism, vague radicalism, romanticism and sentimentality proved to be exactly the concoction the young Germany of the post-war period was longing for. The greatly improved organization of the Party and its untiring efforts to propagandize undoubtedly had much to do with the success of the movement in the later years. And of course it would be idle to deny that the personality of Hitler—like that of Mussolini—his passionate outbursts, his pugnacious and often savage oratory, played a very important part in this success. In contrast with the venerable and rapidly ageing Hindenburg and the mediocrity of the leaders of the Weimar Republic Hitler appeared to many to be the Man of Destiny. And in a country which is only waiting for its deliverer, a legend grows with remarkable speed.

As time went on the attitude of the proprietor class toward the movement also became more favorable, and not infrequently one of direct support. They liked Hitler's aggressive nationalism and, as has been said, they were no longer afraid of his radicalism, especially after he had issued his explanation of the actual meaning of the demand for "the expropriation of land without compensation." The social welfare schemes of the Social Democrats had been costly. The government machinery obviously needed overhauling. "Something must be done." The Hitler movement seemed to be the only alternative, especially if its radicalism could be further tempered by the presence in the Government of such trusted persons as von Papen, Hugenberg and others.

Again the unquestionable decay of the machinery of democratic government should not be overlooked. Hindenburg was clearly showing the effects of old age and had more and more become a figurehead and essentially a tool for the members of a small inner circle. They surrounded the President in Wilhelmstrasse and followed him to his country estate at Neudeck. The von Papen and von Schleicher cabinets which, after the abrupt dismissal of Brüning in May 1932, followed in rapid succession, were of dubious constitutionality. Thirteen years of the Republican régime had strangely failed to produce any outstanding statesman from democratic or Socialist circles. But the military tradition of Prussia was still alive. And as the towering figure of the Fieldmarshal gradually faded away and lost its glamour, the even more formidable figure of the Corporal assumed almost unbelievable proportions and overshadowed Germany's whole political horizon.

THE NATIONAL SOCIALIST STATE

The appointment of Hitler to the office of Reich Chancellor was accompanied by manifestations of enthusiasm similar to those which took place in Rome on October 30, 1922, when Mussolini became the Prime Minister of Italy. Endless columns of the S. A. and S. S. (*Schutz-Stauffel*) men, of the Nationalist *Stahlhelm,* of organizations of young people, and of many other bodies, singing now the "Horst Wessel" song and now the national anthem, moved from every section of Berlin toward the Wilhelmstrasse, where they marched past the new Chancellor and President Hindenburg. And in every other part of Germany like manifestations were taking place.

On the surface Hitler's first cabinet appeared to be rather mild and non-revolutionary. It included, in addition to the Chancellor, only two National Socialists: Frick and Göring. Von Papen was Vice Chancellor and Commissar for Prussia. Hugenberg represented the Nationalists, Seldte, the *Stahlhelm,* conservative organization of ex-service men. Von Neurath and Count Schwerin von Krosigk were retained from the cabinets of von Papen and von Schleicher. The Reichswehr was put under the command of General von Blomberg. The National Socialist State would still seem to be something for the distant future. This was the opinion of many observers who seemed to have overlooked the fact that Hitler could depend on his political machine, and it had already spread the network of its organizations over the entire country. Moreover Frick, as Minister of the Interior of the Reich, and Göring, as Minister of the Interior for Prussia, had under their command all the police force.

The new Government dissolved the Reichstag and new elections took place on March 5, 1933. But in the meantime, on February 27, the building of the Reichstag was found to be afire. The alleged incendiary, a Dutch Communist van der Lubbe, was said to have been caught by the police just as he was about to leave the building. The extraordinary occurrence was declared to have been the signal for a general Communist uprising, an explanation which no one outside Germany has found it possible to believe. The unfortunate van der Lubbe "confessed," was tried, and received the death penalty. And this Reichstag fire was used as a pretext for drastic repressions of both "Marxists" and the Communists. On February 28 the President issued a decree suspending the provisions of the Constitution that guaranteed freedom of speech, of the press, of assembly and the like. The police received practically unlimited powers to deal with offenders against public order and security, and it was in this atmosphere of extreme tension that the elections to the Reichstag took place. The National Socialists obtained 17.3 million votes and 288 seats, and their Nationalist allies, 3.1 million votes and 52 seats. The Social Democrats retained their former total of 120 seats and the Communists won 81 seats, or nineteen less than they had had in the Reichstag of November 1932. The Government was now assured of a 52 per cent majority. The chief issue in the election campaign was the "Enabling Act," and it was duly passed on March 24 by the votes of all parties except the Social Democrats. The Communist and some Social Democrat deputies were either in hiding or in prison and did not take part in the proceedings. The Enabling Act, which was officially known as "A

Law to Combat the Misery of the People and of the Reich," vested in the Government practically unlimited powers for the period of four years. The only restriction on its right to legislate by decrees was a stipulation that no constitutional changes could be made which would affect the position of the Reichstag and the Reichsrat (representing the States). This restriction was in its turn removed by a Law of January 30, 1934.

The Government wasted no time in making full use of such power. The Law of April 7, 1933, provided for the "restoration" of the civil service. By virtue of the law government employees could be removed on the ground that they were "inimical to the State" or "politically undesirable." The Law also contained the Aryan clause which demanded the exclusion from the civil service of all employees of non-German blood. The drastic purge that followed resulted in the removal of a large number of civil servants and, with them, judges whose devotion to National Socialism seemed to be in doubt. A new People's Court, established by a Law of April 24, 1934, was framed in such a way as to place another convenient tool in Government hands. The press, radio, theater and moving pictures were put under the complete control of the Minister of Enlightenment and Propaganda, Dr. Goebbels. The universities and schools were similarly handed over to the care of the Minister of Education, Dr. Rust.

Between March and July 1933 all the other political parties in the Reich passed away. The Communists and the Social Democratic Parties were disbanded and the others went into "voluntary" liquidation. A Law of July 14, 1933, proclaimed that the National Socialist Party was the only one in the Reich and made it a criminal offense to attempt to establish a new party. A short time before, on May 2, the trade unions which had once been pillars of the Social Democratic Party were taken over by the National Socialists. Their leaders were arrested and their newspapers, offices, etc., passed into the hands of the new masters.

The Reichstag was dissolved and new elections took place on November 12. The same day saw a referendum on the Government's policy of withdrawing from the League of Nations and the Disarmament Conference. The National Socialist list—which was the only one—obtained the endorsement of 40.6 million voters, or 92 per cent of the total vote, and the foreign policy of the Government polled 39.6 million votes. The interpreting of these huge figures, of course, should be done with much caution, but it cannot reasonably be doubted that the Government was not lacking in support. By a Law of December 1, 1933, the National Socialist Party was officially incorporated in the machinery of the State.

Even more drastic perhaps were the measures designed to give political unity to the Reich and abolish the federal system. Already previous to the passing of the Enabling Law, or between March 5 and 16, 1933, each of the States of the Reich was put under a *Reichskommissar*. By a Law of April 7, 1933, the duties of every *Reichskommissar* were taken over by a *Statthalter,* who was a personal representative of Hitler and appointed on his recommendation, by the President. A *Statthalter* is also vested with practically dictatorial powers.

The Law of January 30, 1934, dealt the last blow to local autonomy. The sovereign rights of the States were transferred to the Reich and the state governments were subordinated to the Government of the Reich. The Reich Minister of the Interior was to administer them through the particular *Statthalter* in authority. Although the state governments continued to exist their autonomy was completely gone. The logical next step was (by a law of February 14, 1934) to abolish the *Reichsrat,* which, to repeat, was made up of the representatives of the States. All these measures, however, are considered to be only provisional, and the final constitution of the centralized and unified Germany is still in process of preparation.

An important element in local administration is the holding of the office of *Statthalter* and that of *Gauleiter* by the same person. The National Socialist Party has divided the whole country into territorial units known as *Gaue,* and the *Gauleiter* is the chief officer of the *Gau.* The personal union of the office of *Statthalter* and *Gauleiter* established a direct link between the local administration and the Party. In Germany, as in Italy, the Party completely controls the entire administrative and political structure. "The National Socialist movement," Hitler declared at Nuremberg in September 1933, "is the German Reich. It is the State." The Law of January 30, 1935, on the government of the communes (*Gemeindeordnung*) embodied this principle. It provided that the mayor and his adjutant must enjoy the confidence of the Party and of the State (*werden durch das Vertrauen von Partei und Staat in ihr Amt berufen*) and made it their duty to keep in close touch with the local representative of the Party.

The supreme executive and legislative power in this coordinated and unified Germany is concentrated in the hands of Adolf Hitler, Chancellor of the Reich and leader of the National Socialist Party. On August 2, 1934, on the death of Hindenberg, he also became President of the Reich; this office was conferred upon him by a law issued by the Government of which he was himself the head. The decision, however, was submitted on August 19 to a referendum in which 39 million voted for Hitler and 4 million against him. Following as it did upon the tragic and bloody events of June 30, when von Schleicher, his wife, Röhm, a number of S. A. leaders and many others lost their lives, and upon the murder of Dollfuss in July, this expression of confidence in Hitler was certainly not lacking in impressiveness, even if full allowance is made for possibilities of direct and indirect pressure inherent in such plebiscites. The Weimar Constitution, of which the liberal Germans used to be so proud, has not as yet been officially discarded, but it certainly has been put to a use which its framers could never have foreseen. Amid the ruins of the Weimar structure the Chancellor and Führer, as Hitler continues to be called, is both in law and in fact just as much the supreme and undisputed master of Germany as Mussolini, a nominal appointee of the King, is the supreme and undisputed master of Italy.

THE FASCIST AND THE NATIONAL SOCIALIST REVOLUTIONS

Fascism and National Socialism both aspire to the honor of having accomplished a revolution. The validity of this claim has sometimes been questioned. It is pointed out that, among other things, they reached power and made their constitutional changes by legal or quasi-legal means, although no one has denied that without the organized armed force at their disposal their aims could not have been achieved. The substitution, for a parliamentary monarchy and a democratic republic, of a personal dictatorship based on a party machine controlling the entire State administration may on good grounds be held to constitute a revolution. The change in the form of government was accompanied by much violence and brutality, by the forcible annihilation of the opposition, and by the removal from office of a number of officials. In this respect, however, both Italy and Germany fall short of the classic example set by the Russian Revolution. As an astute observer

living in Berlin remarked to me, one could hardly
speak of a real German revolution in the case of a
change in the form of government where the new-
comers retain in their service practically the entire
police force of Prussia. After three years of National
Socialist rule von Papen, von Neurath and Count
Schwerin von Krosigk are still among the councillors
of the régime, and Dr. Schacht is more powerful
than ever. From this point of view the situation in
Italy is very similar. Even more significant perhaps
is the retention of the general social structure which
existed before Fascism and National Socialism came
into power. Although, as will later be shown, the
control of the State over finance, industry and the
landlords has been drastically extended, there has
been so far no sharp and definite breach with the
past. Private ownership as the basis of the totalitarian State has proved to be more than an empty
phrase. Neither Italy nor Germany has as yet experienced the colossal social and economic upheaval
which was the fate of Imperial Russia. The majority
of the Italian and German upper and middle classes
are today in a position which is not vastly different
from what it was before the advent to power of
Fascism and National Socialism. This, of course, refers to the economic and social status of these
groups and leaves out of consideration the restrictions imposed upon any manifestations of intellectual and political freedom. And yet, although the
Fascist and the National Socialist revolutions are
perhaps not worthy of the name when compared

with the more thorough and drastic experiment carried through by the Soviets in Russia, they have nevertheless brought to the life of the two countries so many novel and vital elements that one certainly hesitates to describe them as mere changes in the form of government. To an outsider their claims to having given the world an entirely new social and political philosophy seem ridiculously exaggerated. But the work of domestic reconstruction accomplished by Mussolini and Hitler is bound to leave a lasting imprint on the future development of Italy and Germany, and, for all we know, that may be only the first step toward further and more far-reaching readjustments. Neither movement, of course, claims to have reached anything like its final stage.

CHAPTER III

THE ARTICLES OF FAITH

THE NEW CREED

Fascism and National Socialism both claim to be much more than mere forms of government. "Like all sound political conceptions," writes Mussolini, "Fascism is action and it is thought. . . . Fascism is not only a law-giver and founder of institutions, it is also an educator and a promoter of spiritual life. It aims to refashion both the outward form of life and also its inward content—man, his character and his beliefs. To achieve this purpose it enforces discipline and uses authority. It enters into the soul and rules with undisputed sway. Therefore it has chosen as its emblem the lictor's rod, the symbol of unity, strength and justice." Hitler takes a no less solemn view of his movement. He declared that National Socialism is "a heroic doctrine which brings out the value of blood, race and personality as well as the eternal laws of natural selection (*Auslesegesetz*) and finds itself in an avowed and irreconcilable opposition to the philosophy of the pacifist international democracy and to its products (*Auswirkungen*)." Mussolini maintains, moreover, that the influence of Fascism is by no means limited to Italy. "Fascism,

56

as an idea, a doctrine, a realization, is universal; it is Italian in its particular institutions, but it is universal in the spirit, nor could it be otherwise. The spirit is universal by reason of its nature."

It is hardly necessary to say that to an outsider the prophetic and the oracular in Mussolini and Hitler appear to be based on a very flimsy foundation. Their teachings, to begin with, are extremely loose and uncertain in some essential parts. This undoubtedly contributed in no small degree to the success of the Fascist and National Socialist movements: the less precise and definite the slogan and the program, the wider the appeal. It will be remembered that while the program of the National Socialist Party was declared in 1926 to be "unchangeable" it was officially explained that this applied only to the fundamental principles, and not to the methods by which the latter were to be put into practice; some of the principles were anything but clear and concrete. Even today they are open to innumerable interpretations. This is particularly true of the economic policies of National Socialism and, in a lesser degree, of Fascism. To be rigidly doctrinaire is, moreover, repugnant to the spirit of these movements. Mussolini maintains, for instance, that "Fascism should be revised, corrected, enlarged, developed." Under these conditions it is by no means easy to be sure that the views of even the leaders themselves expressed some time ago represent the opinion of the Party now.

No intellectual movement is entirely independent,

and a number of influences have been suggested as
having left their imprint upon the teachings of Fascism and National Socialism. Mussolini is said to
owe much to Machiavelli, Schopenhauer, Nietzsche,
Renan, Blanqui, Georges Sorel, William James,
Bergson and Pareto. The antecedents of National
Socialism have been traced to Luther, Kant, Hegel,
Fichte, Friedrich List, de Gobineau, H. S. Chamber-
lain and, of course, to Mussolini himself. Many of
these affiliations have been clearly established or
even openly acknowledged. Nevertheless the com-
bination of the various elements, none of them absolutely original, in the philosophy of Fascism and
National Socialism, bears the distinct marks of their
respective leaders and presents a system of thought
which, if rather obscure, is fairly comprehensive.

It would seem that the vogue of the new cults
arises in part from the already traditional and almost "ritualistic" terminology in which the writings
of the Fascists and National Socialists are clothed.
The written works and speeches of Mussolini and
Hitler and of many of their followers have not lent
themselves readily to interpretation in plain English. National Socialism has in particular distinguished itself by evolving a new vernacular which
specializes in spinning endless and bizarre words into
endless and even more bizarre sentences, often to say
very little indeed. A non-believer who attacks these
verbose monuments of pagan theology certainly
needs courage and perseverance.

THE NATION AND THE STATE

One of the fundamental ideas of Fascism is the supremacy of the State. "Anti-individualistic, the Fascist conception of life," writes Mussolini, "stresses the importance of the State. It accepts the individual only in so far as his interests coincide with those of the State. And it stands for the conscience and the universal will of man as an historic entity. . . . The Fascist conception of the State is all-embracing. Beyond it no human or spiritual concepts can exist, much less have value." This principle is summarized in the well-known watchword: 'All in the State, nothing outside the State, nothing against the State.' "

The "totalitarian" State of Fascism is endorsed by the National Socialists. In either case it is accompanied by a violent denunciation of democracy in the struggle against which the two movements have fought relentlessly. *Mein Kampf* is full of invectives against parliamentarism and against democratic institutions in general; for they put their faith not in quality, but in numbers. "Democratic régimes," writes Mussolini, "may be described as those under which the people are, from time to time, deluded into the belief that they exercise sovereignty. . . . Democracy is a kingless régime infested by many kings who are sometimes more exclusive, more tyrannical, and destructive than one, even if he be a tyrant."

The totalitarian State is not simply an abstraction devised for the purpose of disguising the political dictatorship of Fascism and National Socialism. It is supposed to be the vehicle through which the higher conception of the Nation finds its external manifestation. The Nation is just as exacting as the totalitarian State. "The individual is nothing— *das Volk* is everything!" according to a statement by Hitler. And the German conception of *das Volk* comprises elements which are entirely alien to the Italian idea of the Nation. The Hitler conception of nationality is in theory deeply rooted in racial, biological and ethnographical concepts. It is based on the assumption of the superiority of the Nordic race, the purest representatives of which are believed to be the Germans. Hitler, Rosenberg, Goebbels, Streicher and the other leaders of the movement have devoted much space in their writings and speeches to the glorification of the Nordic virtues. The question of "blood" is in the forefront of the National Socialist program. The totalitarian State they are trying to build is to be based on the principle of race. It will be a national community of people of the same racial stock to the exclusion of all "non-Aryan" elements. "The science of the race is our German Gospel," Heinrich Himmler, the leader of the S. S. troops, declared in the summer of 1935 in a speech which was given much prominence in the German press. The scientific shallowness of this doctrine is so obvious that it hardly needs to be emphasized. Its application in practice presents insurmountable obstacles, since to arrive at any minute determination of the racial sources of the population of Central Europe, or of any other part of the world, is an entirely hopeless task. In Germany herself the racial policy of the National Socialist Government has been reduced for all practical purposes to a relentless and systematic persecution of the Jews and of all those who have any drop of Jewish blood in their veins. All members of the Party and of its affiliated agencies, all civil servants and the employees of many private concerns have been requested to prepare family trees going back several generations, and these are carefully scrutinized by learned "experts." The discovery, sometimes quite unexpected, of a grandmother or other ancestor whose Aryan origin was open to doubt has been the cause of the ruin of more than one promising career. The same principle, as will appear later, is now being enforced in the land policy of the National Socialist Government. Daily reminders of this strange obsession from which Germany is suffering today may be seen in the neat little folders bearing the legend "My Ancestors" which are displayed in the windows of practically every stationery store throughout the land. Some are in expensive leather bindings, but many are cheap little things which can be purchased for a few pfennigs. I was strongly urged to buy one by a friendly and enthusiastic salesman who was surprised and grieved by my firm refusal.

Mussolini, too, has spoken of the Nation in terms that have been interpreted by German writers as an endorsement of their racial theory. This interpreta-

tion is a distinct mistake. "The Italian Nation is
an organism having aims, a life and means superior
in power and duration to the single individual com-
posing it," says the opening paragraph of the Italian
Charter of Labor. "It is a moral, political and economic entity which finds its integral realization in
the Fascist State." The Italian Nation as understood by the leader of Fascism, however, is something very different from the National Socialist conception of race. In an interview with Emil Ludwig,
Mussolini declared that "race . . . is a feeling and
not a reality; 95 per cent a feeling." And this sen-
tence has since been reprinted in an official Italian
publication under the Duce's own signature. The
Italian conception of the Nation is, if not more
scientific, at least far less objectionable than that of
Hitler. It would seem to be a romantic idealization
of the Roman tradition, of Rome as "the palpitating
heart of Imperial Italy," of Rome as "a political
conception, not a race but an animating spirit," to
quote Professor Gioacchino Volpe. "Rome is our
point of departure and our reference," wrote Mussolini, ". . . We dream of a Roman Italy, of an Italy
wise and strong, disciplined and imperial. Much of
the immortal spirit of Rome has been revived in
Fascism. Roman are our lictor's rods, Roman is our
fighting organization, Roman is our pride and our
courage: *Civis romanus sum*. . . . The Romans
were not only warriors but also formidable construc-
tors who could defy and did defy time. In the war
and in victory Italy was Roman for the first time in

fifteen centuries." This theory of the Nation as a spiritual conception and not as a racial entity is a fundamental and significant difference between Fascism and National Socialism. Its practical consequence is the absence in Italy of any anti-Jewish movement. German anti-Semitism, of course, is not merely the creation of Adolf Hitler. It also has its historical and social roots. But the personal opinions of the supreme leader in a totalitarian State are of paramount importance, and no reasonable person could possibly doubt that the Chancellor and Führer must bear the full burden of responsibility for the treatment to which the Jews have been subjected in the Reich. To this I shall return in a later chapter.

HIERARCHY AND NATIONAL SOLIDARITY

Having proclaimed the supremacy of the Nation and of the State, and rejected democracy as a form of government, Fascism and National Socialism must inevitably repudiate the principle on which parliamentary government is based. "Fascism denies that the majority, by the simple fact that it is a majority, can direct human society," writes Mussolini, "it denies that numbers alone can govern by means of periodical consultations, and it affirms the immutable, beneficent and fruitful inequality of mankind, an inequality which can never permanently be turned into equality by the mere operation of a mechanical process such as universal suffrage." This idea, which is fully shared by the National

Socialists, in itself leads the two movements toward the acceptance of that principle of hierarchy and leadership which implies, in the words of Hitler, "the absolute authority of the leaders over those below and their responsibility to those above." Parliamentary rule, which is represented as a squabble of selfish interests for power, is to give place to the rule by an *élite* bound by a strict discipline and embodying the highest aspirations of the Nation. Hitler extols this restoration of the "unity of the spirit and the will of the German people." Mussolini declares that he "who speaks of hierarchy says discipline."

Government by an *élite* is not in itself an objectionable principle. This is, I think, what democracy is striving to achieve through the machinery of general elections. That the procedure has not always been successful will be readily admitted. But what have Fascism and National Socialism to offer in place of the despised methods of democracy? To this all-important question they give no definite answer. In theory the leaders are, presumably, brought forth by the workings of the law of natural selection. In practice, however, as we know, this merely means the hegemony of the political party which has seized power and has ruthlessly stamped out all opposition. Ernest Raue, following in the footsteps of other German writers, rightly observes that in the last analysis the entire doctrine of Fascism and National Socialism must be traced to the will of their leaders. It is the will of the leaders, again, that determines who shall form that *élite* which will hold in its hands the destinies of the country. Raue's little book, which is a glorification of this and similar principles, not only won him the degree of Doctor of Social Sciences in the University of Berlin but has also had wide circulation.

It is, moreover, maintained by Italian and German writers that hierarchy and *élite* principles are by no means incompatible with "real" liberty. So long as the State and the Party are the representatives of the Nation and the mouthpieces of national interests the liberties of the citizen are fully safeguarded. "Far from crushing the individual," writes Mussolini, "the Fascist State multiplies his energies, just as in a regiment a soldier is not diminished but multiplied by the number of his fellow soldiers." The individual is free, it is claimed, so long as he has performed his duty to the State, and as duties to the State have an unquestioned priority, no conflict between the "real" interests of the individual and the interests of the State is possible. It is only through the State that the individual can achieve complete self-expression. "Freedom is not a right, it is a duty," writes Mussolini. "It is not a gift, it is a conquest. It is not equality, it is privilege. The concept of freedom changes with the passing of time. There is a freedom in time of peace which is not freedom in time of war. There is a freedom in times of prosperity which is not a freedom that can be tolerated in times of poverty." It is the protection offered to the individual by the State, which is the only real guarantee of his freedom. Hitler, too, de-

clared that "one must not always speak of the
rights; one must also speak of the duties" of the individual. This conception of the duty of the citizen
to the State is given immense prominence in Germany today and the word *Pflicht* is one of the most
abused words in the German language. The whole
concept of hierarchy and of the obligations of the
individual to the State have a distinctly militaristic
flavor, which cannot but be pleasing to those who
were brought up in the Prussian tradition. Mussolini is quoted by Dr. Goebbels as having declared
that "Fascism is the Roman version of Prussianism
(*römisches Preussentum*)" which is, broadly speaking, true so far as the principles underlying the two
conceptions of the State are concerned. But the vast
differences in the psychologies of the two countries
have not been much diminished, I think, even by
thirteen years of Fascist rule.

The subordination of the interests of the individual to those of the State or of the community plays
a very prominent part in the theories of Fascism and
National Socialism. "Fascists . . . ," writes Mussolini, "think of life in terms of duty and struggle and
conquest. They feel that life should be high and
full, lived for oneself, but above all for others—for
those who are at hand and those who are far distant,
for our contemporaries, and for those who will come
after us." The same idea is tersely expressed in the
motto of the Program of the National Socialist
Party: *"Gemeinnutz vor Eigennutz,"* "the interests
of all before the interests of one." This is the corner

stone of the concept of "national solidarity," of that *Gemeinschaft* which is one of the chief objectives of the totalitarian State. It has a strong appeal to the sentimental side of the German character and is used effectively. In his address opening the Winter Relief campaign of 1934, a campaign that was carried on under the slogan of "national solidarity," Hitler strongly stressed the fact that it was not enough to contribute to the campaign fund; the contribution should be made in such a manner as to mean a real sacrifice for the giver. "If the entire Nation realizes that the relief measures we are taking involve an actual sacrifice for every one," he declared, "then these measures will serve not merely to relieve material needs but they will also achieve something far more important. They will make one realize that the national community (*Volksgemeinschaft*) is not a mere empty concept, but an actual living one."

National solidarity is also the denial of class struggle. Mussolini and Hitler both won their spurs in fighting the red menace. Nothing more natural for them, therefore, than to reject the Marxian interpretation of history. Here again, however, as in the case of their definitions of what is meant by the concept of the Nation, there is a significant difference in its interpretation by the two leaders. Mussolini had long been an ardent Socialist. When he was expelled from the Socialist Party in 1914 he declared that he would remain a Socialist even if he had lost his membership card. He has travelled far in the last twenty years and today he rejects the class struggle as the great moving power of human society. But he still believes that there is a conflict of interests between capital and labor. This conflict however is not irremediable, as is thought by the Marxian Socialists. On the contrary, the interests of the two parties can be reconciled and it is the duty of the totalitarian State to see to it that an amiable solution is brought about. This is exactly the purpose of the corporate organization that has been painstakingly built up in Italy since 1926. On the other hand, Hitler, the son of a modest government employee, had to work for a time as a manual laborer. He gives in *Mein Kampf* a vivid and unhappy picture of the conditions of life of the proletariat. In spite of this experience he held himself altogether aloof from the official Socialist *mots d'ordre*. National Socialism, therefore, not only rejects class struggle as a great historical force but also denies that there is any necessary conflict of interests between capital and labor. If such conflict existed under German capitalism it was merely the effect of the greed and stupidity of the ruling classes of the "Liberal-Marxist" State. Under the benign influence of the National Socialist régime, it is held, they must and will disappear.

ITALIAN AND GERMAN "SOCIALISM"

The conception of national solidarity determines the attitude of Fascism and National Socialism toward economic problems. The course they have chosen is a middle one between capitalism and socialism. Article 7 of the Charter of Labor declares that "private interest in the sphere of production is the most effective and useful instrument in the interest of the Nation." This also expresses the National Socialist view. The right of private property is thus maintained, but the exercise of this right is subject to the control of the State, which reserves the power to intervene at any moment and direct private initiative into the channels which it considers desirable. Sombart has stated that the economic organization of Fascism is "the highest synthesis of State power and authority compatible with the capitalist system." The argument is advanced that in the German totalitarian State the employer is no longer the "hereditary enemy of labor" but has been transformed into one of the "soldiers of the mighty Labor Front (*Arbeitsfront*) of the German people," and as such is doing his duty in the service of the Nation. It will be shown in a later chapter to what extent this statement is justified by the changes that have actually taken place in the position of the employers. The general principles of the Fascist and National Socialist policy toward capital and labor are briefly set forth by Hitler in a speech delivered in March 1935: "The people do not live for economic organization (*Wirtschaft*) and economic organization does not exist for capital, but capital is the servant of economic organization and economic organization is the servant of the people."

This is a formula that is both broad and obscure. It is like a promise and a menace, and it may prove to be both or neither.

Little need here be said about other important economic principles that appear in the program of the National Socialist Party: the expropriation of land without compensation for public purposes, the elimination of interest on agricultural debts and of speculation in land values, the nationalization of trusts, public ownership of department stores, profit-sharing in the case of large concerns, and the abolition of the "slavery of interest." All these demands, of course, continue to form a theoretical part of the official program. And some of them, it will be seen, have not remained dead letters. The most puzzling of all is the question of the abolition of the "slavery of interest." The real meaning of this mysterious and ominous phrase is still a matter of conjecture. Interpretations range from the complete nationalization of all banks, the abolition of unearned income and the cancellation of all debts to the most innocuous explanations. It has been suggested, for instance, that the abolition of the "slavery of interest" really means that "every one should pay his debts and make no new ones"!

The socialist tendencies of Fascism and National Socialism have also found their expression in their attitude toward labor. Article 2 of the Italian Charter of Labor declares that "work in all its forms—intellectual, technical and manual—both organizing and executive, is a social duty." National Socialism enthusiastically accepts this principle and maintains that it is not only the duty of every citizen to work, but also his right. Hitler has stated that while every German was under obligation to contribute by his work to the general advancement of the Nation, it was, more than that, his right to demand that the government should provide him with the ways and means of finding a place and purpose for his labor. "Work and Bread" (*Arbeit und Brot*) has been one of the Nation's slogans, and it has been the moving power behind the Government's program of fighting unemployment. There has also been much talk about the dignity of labor. It has been extolled in glowing terms by Mussolini, Hitler and their lieutenants. Hitler's dictum, "Honor work and respect the worker" was treated as if it were a revelation. And the passages from *Mein Kampf* which proclaim that the happiness and contentment of the worker are conditions on which depend development and progress of business enterprise and the success of the employer himself were reproduced in innumerable articles and pamphlets, with comments which would seem to imply that no such thing could be possible under the Liberal-Marxist régime!

Considerable attention is also paid by Fascism and National Socialism to the situation of the tiller of the soil. It is deemed essential to improve the condition of the rural class and to promote farming not only for reasons of economic expediency—both Italy and Germany are striving hard to become self-sufficient in foodstuffs—but also as a matter of social policy. The totalitarian State thinks in terms of a balanced economy in which a certain ratio between the urban and the rural population will be maintained. The excessive industrialization of Germany in pre-war years is believed to be responsible for many of her present economic evils, for social unrest and the growth of Communism up to 1933. The movement back to the farm, it is argued, will restore the traditional balance of the German people; it will also contribute powerfully to the rejuvenation of the race by relieving the congestion of overcrowded urban tenements and will give further generations a better chance to grow and develop in the healthy surroundings of the countryside. "Blood and Land" —*Blut und Boden*—is another National Socialist watchword of far-reaching importance.

THE HEROIC ELEMENT

I have already pointed out that Fascism and National Socialism claim to be new philosophies, almost new religions. The heroic and idealistic part of their teachings therefore must not be disregarded. Their glorification of the State and the Nation leads them along the path of extreme militarism. Mussolini derives much of his inspiration from the martial heritage of ancient Rome. Hitler draws his from Germany's Teutonic forefathers and the Prussian Army. "Fascism . . .," writes Mussolini, "believes neither in the possibility nor in the usefulness of perpetual peace. War alone brings to its highest tension all human energy and puts the stamp of nobility upon the people who have the courage to engage in it." Hitler has advanced very similar views. "No one can doubt that in the future the world will witness tremendous battles for the existence of mankind," he says in *Mein Kampf;* "in the long run only the passion for self-preservation can win a lasting victory. When confronted with it, so-called humanitarianism, that product of a mixture of stupidity, cowardice and superciliousness, will melt away like snow in the March sunshine. In everlasting battles mankind has achieved greatness —in everlasting peace it would be doomed to destruction." These ideas permeate the entire social and political structure of the two States. We have already seen that the Italian Fascist Party officially describes itself as a "civil Militia." The militarist spirit of the two movements is undoubtedly due to the fact that they are products of the aftermath of the war. Mussolini, it will be remembered, had been the leader of the "interventionists" both before and after the war. Hitler began his political career as a champion of that German army which, it was alleged, had been "stabbed in the back" by traitors behind the firing line. The bulk of the followers of Fascism and National Socialism in the early days were drawn from the men who were demobilized from the army. Even today a war record is the best

introduction to Party officials and the best qualifications for a Party office.

According to Fascism and National Socialism war
is not only the supreme test of the Nation but also
the most sublime of experiences for the individual.
National Socialist leaders have repeated over and
over again that war is for the man what child-birth
is for the woman. "Fascism believes . . . in holi-
ness and in heroism," writes Mussolini, "that is to
say in actions influenced by no economic motive,
direct or indirect." And it rejects with contempt
the materialistic concept of happiness. "Fascism
denies the validity of the equation well-being=hap-
piness which would reduce men to the level of
animals, caring for one thing only—to be fat and
well fed. It would degrade humanity to a purely
physical existence." War occupies the very opposite
end of the scale of values. It is in the supreme sacrifice of personal interest, comforts and life itself
that the idea of national solidarity and of the supremacy of the Nation finds its highest expression.
Contempt for purely material aims is preached today in Italy and Germany with remarkable candor
and truly religious fervor. "Remember," said Mussolini in 1930, addressing the Young Fascists, "that
Fascism does not promise you honors or rewards,
but only duty and fighting." And these are the
promises that raise the youthful Spartans of modern
Italy to the highest pitch of enthusiasm. For
Fascism, as well as National Socialism, is above all
a heroic doctrine.

THE DOCTRINE AND THE RANK AND FILE

Assuming that the foregoing survey of the fundamental ideas of Fascism and National Socialism
gives a sufficiently accurate summary of their teaching, it will be readily admitted that the new philosophy contains little to afford a rational explanation
of the amazing success of the movements themselves
either in Italy or in Germany. The claims of Mussolini and Hitler to foremost places among the spiritual leaders of mankind is not borne out by an
examination of their contribution to human thought.
The secret of their success therefore must be sought
not in their philosophy, which contains little that is
new and even less that is convincing, but rather in
the historical, political, economic and social conditions of the post-war period which paved the way for
their triumph. It was the appeal to the emotions
and not to reason that made Fascism and National
Socialism what they are today. Their ideology nevertheless is the daily bread of some 43 million Italians and 64 million Germans, and it is being dis-
seminated with an energy and persistency that no
other government, except perhaps that of Soviet
Russia, has ever displayed before—and this with a
technique greatly superior to that of the U.S.S.R.
It would be a fascinating study to attempt to discover what the supporters of Mussolini and Hitler
really think of the fundamentals of the régime they
are helping to establish. I cannot claim to have
made any such study which moreover, for obvious

reasons, is not feasible. But during visits to Italy in 1935 and to Germany in 1934 and 1935 I made a practice of asking Italians and Germans whom I had a chance to meet to tell me what, in their opinion, represents the essence of the philosophy of their national government. Such casual conversation, needless to say, offers no real ground for broad generalizations. Nevertheless the answers I received proved to be interesting and sometimes illuminating.

There are obviously a large number of people in both Italy and Germany who are opposed to their present governments, and their criticism is no less unsparing, if more discreet, than that we are used to outside their frontiers. Discreet though it be, criticism of this kind is much more frequent and outspoken than the outsider usually imagines. In Italy, where Fascism has been at the helm for thirteen years, the ranks of the Party have inevitably absorbed certain elements whose attitude toward the régime is in certain cases lukewarm and in others even hostile. I have heard men wearing in their lapels the Fascist badge, which is compulsory for members of the Party, denounce Mussolini with a bitterness which no political émigré could possibly excel. And I was told that their membership in the Party was a necessity which made them feel ashamed of themselves.

The attitude of such people, whose personal tragedy cannot but inspire the deepest sympathy, may have no special value for the present discussion, since it is an attitude necessarily similar to that of the many critics of Fascism and National Socialism abroad. Moreover, what I was trying to get was some glimpse of the reasoning which makes the masses of the people rally to the lictor's rods and the swastika. It was therefore from men and women who were in one way or another associated with the respective régimes that I attempted to obtain my information. There is probably a considerable percentage among them who have bowed to necessity and are serving Fascism and National Socialism because Fascism and National Socialism are now their masters, and because any sign of opposition might get them into the most serious trouble. But far the greatest number, I think, are supporting the régime because they have found in it certain elements which they can endorse. One of the advantages of political and social doctrine that partakes of many elements is that it offers opportunities to its followers to concentrate on certain phases only and to disregard altogether or at least thrust into the background those which they find particularly unpalatable.

The discussions I had with Italians over a bottle of *Chianti* in some backstreet *trattoria* or with Germans over a glass of *Würzburger* in a *Bierhalle* brought out very clearly the fundamental difference in the attitude of the two peoples. The Italians, as a rule, do not take the official doctrine of Fascism too seriously. Except for the learned and the academic who produce elaborate volumes on the theory of the Corporate State, they usually dismiss the subject with general comments on·Mussolini's genius, the remarkable progress Italy has made under his rule, the improvement in public services and building activities, the progress of physical education or some kindred matter, which would seem to betray an interest in the concrete results obtained, rather than in the metaphysical aspects of Fascism.

Even high government officials in charge of the important policies of the régime frequently discuss Fascism's theoretical aspects in a manner which, while very witty and entertaining, is a better proof of their delightful sense of·humor than of any blind bowing down to Fascist Truth. The young people, with whom the Duce is immensely popular, seem to be more interested in football and skiing than in the moral principles underlying the Charter of Labor. Who would blame them for that? The glorification of the régime in Mussolini's passionate rhetoric is not incompatible with a certain carefully measured degree of self-criticism. After thirteen years of its rule Fascism, I think, is willing to look upon itself in a manner that is not wholly uncritical. It is proud of what it considers to be its achievements, but it does not completely shut its eyes to its shortcomings. Freedom from dogmatism and a keen sense of humor have always been among the most attractive aspects of the Italian character. It is by no means certain that the Duce himself does not sympathize with this attitude. Did he not for years keep the movement from any dogmatic entanglement as a "free body of athletic men"?

The Germans take their National Socialist philosophy or *Weltanschauung* in much more serious vein. This may be due partly to the fact that Hitler's road to power was longer, his struggle more stubborn and partly to the fact that his tenure of office has been shorter than Mussolini's. But the real explanation is probably to be found in German character itself and that attitude toward life in which duty (*Pflicht*) in the sense of dogma sanctified by the proper authority plays so important a part. The *Weltanschauung* is duly canonized and is the subject of learned lectures in schools and universities and of innumerable discussions in the organizations of the Party and its various subsidiaries. Nevertheless it should not be thought that the intricacies of the National Socialist theology have already penetrated deeply into the mind of the rank and file. The usual answer to the question "What, in your opinion, is the essence of the *Weltanschauung?*" was that this was a very difficult thing to explain. Some of the members of the National Socialist Party displayed no more interest in its ideology than did many of the Italian Fascists in the ideology of Fascism. But even among those who had pondered over the writings of the National Socialist prophets or received the proper schooling in the teachings of Hitler, Goebbels, Rosenberg and Streicher there is a considerable divergence of view as to what constitutes the kernel of the new philosophy. One hears, of course, invariable references to the achievements of the régime, to the elimination of the Communist

danger, the reduction of unemployment, the resump-
tion by Germany of her place as a great military
Power. The intense nationalism and the heroic aspect of National Socialism make a strong appeal to
many, and at least on one occasion I was told that
the "liberation" of Germany from the Jews was the
real and the highest aim of the Hitler movement.
This remark came from a magnificent-looking young
man in a black S. S. uniform. Among the younger
generation there is also a very definite tendency to
dwell on the presumably unlimited possibilities for
national betterment resulting from unified leadership and the creation of a "common will." My very
definite impression from contacts with the local officials of the National Socialist Party is that many
of them are sincerely and deeply engrossed in the
work of social and economic rehabilitation in which
the present Government is very active, and that to
them this effort to improve the lot of the less fortunate members of the community represents the very
essence of the *Weltanschauung*. I tried to argue, in
answer, that there was no necessary connection between such commendable efforts and the theory of
the race and National Socialist dictatorship in general. They would not listen to me, of course, and
invariably replied that National Socialism is suc-
ceeding where democracy failed, which, historically,
is probably not true.

The older generation, including some of the vast
army of government officials, finds itself in a more
difficult position since it has been brought up in

ideas that are different in more than one respect from those of Germany's present rulers. These people, I think, try hard to restore their moral balance by concentrating on the nationalist parts of the Hitler philosophy, on the principle of national solidarity and the sacrifice of one's individual interests to those of the Nation. This is why one finds, neatly framed on the wall of so many German offices and homes, the following verses ascribed, wrongly I am told, to Fichte:

Du sollst an Deutschlands Zukunft glauben,
an deines Volkes Auferstehen.
Lass diesen Glauben dir nicht rauben
trotz allem, was geschehen.

Und handeln sollst du so, als hinge
vor dir und deinem Tun allein
das Schicksal ab der deutschen Dinge,
und die Verantwortung wär dein.

Of this poem the following is a free translation:

Believe in the future of Germany;
in your people's resurrection.
Undismayed, believe;
in spite of all that may befall.

With unwavering courage
act as though on you and on what you do
depends Germany's high destiny;
as though you alone were responsible
and the fate of the Fatherland in your hand.

By giving prominence to the nationalist sentimentality of Fichte, if Fichte's it was, it is possible to
dismiss from one's mind the intolerance and harsh-
ness of the race theory and to try to forget the brutality and violence of the National Socialist methods
by treating them as merely one passing manifestation of a revolutionary crisis. It would be unwise to
assume, however, that sentimentality dominates the
interpretation of the *Weltanschauung* which is
pumped into the heads of hundreds of thousands of
young Germans by booted and uniformed officials
in military and semi-military camps. Here ideas of
race and nationalist intolerance hold their place side
by side with the exaltation of the supremacy of the
State and national solidarity and, indeed, weld into
one and the same doctrine. And it is largely on the
attitude of these rising generations that the future
course of Germany depends.

CHAPTER IV

THE ORGANS OF ECONOMIC CONTROL

THE END OF ECONOMIC LIBERALISM

THE element of vagueness and uncertainty which characterizes the teaching of Fascism and National Socialism persists when one turns to the examination of their economic and social institutions. Although the beginnings of the Corporate State in Italy may be traced back to 1926 and perhaps even earlier, and although the Italian experiment has created a vast literature, the structure Mussolini is building up is still by no means completed. Until 1934 Italy was a Corporate State without corporations. It was only by the law of February 5, 1934, that the corporations were officially established. In the summer of 1935 they were still in an embryonic stage, some of them existed merely on paper and discussion as to the form and functions of the new institutions was as keen as ever. The provisional character and imperfection of the present corporate organization is admitted in Rome. In the Via Vittorio Veneto, the very heart of the new section of the city, stands the magnificent modernist-style building of the Ministry of Corporations. On the walls of its reception room the Charter of Labor has been traced in mosaics in the midst of a sumptuous decorative design in which the lictor's rods occupy a predominant place. But the affable and courteous officials who put themselves at the complete disposal of the foreign visitor and shower upon him publications in various foreign languages dealing with corporate activities, somewhat surprise him by the polite but firm statement that, although the Ministry of Corporations has been in existence for a number of years, the Corporate State itself is still largely a thing of the future. To reproduce this statement is perhaps no gross indiscretion since the Duce in an address before the joint meeting of the councils of the 22 corporations in November 1934 declared that "we are still at the starting point, not at the point of arrival." The organization therefore is admittedly tentative and subject to further readjustment.

The situation in Germany is even less certain. The country is still in the early stages of the process of reconstruction, and much that exists at present is bound either to disappear or to be completely remodelled. There is a considerable degree of disagreement within the Fascist and the National Socialist Parties as to the methods and even as to some of the principles on which their economic and social policies are to be based. The new legislation is often clothed in such involved and abstract phraseology that to ascertain its real meaning is anything but an easy task. Not infrequently it is permissive and not mandatory, and it would be risky to assume that this or that novel institution discussed with a wealth of detail in a verbose decree does really exist. With all these reservations the general framework of the institutions Italy and Germany are trying to set up may be regarded as reasonably clear. With the principles on which they are based we are already familiar. Chief among them is that of the supremacy of the Nation and of the State over the individual, and the subordination of individual and class interests to those of the community. In his speech before the National Council of Corporations on November 14, 1934, Mussolini declared that on the day the Grand Council of Fascism was established in 1923 political liberalism was buried. "Today," he added, referring to the bill providing for the establishment of corporations which was under discussion, "we are burying economic liberalism." This is to be accomplished through the intervention of the State, with the preservation at the same time of the rights of private property and private initiative; for, it will be remembered, they are the very foundation of the present interpretation of the economic programs of Fascism and National Socialism. The intervention of the State, however, would consist mainly in the organization of the economic forces of the country for the best interests of all and would be free from bureaucratism and monopolies, which are associated with Socialism. The "end of economic liberalism" thus interpreted, would seem to be reduced to the supervision of private interests by the State, which is not fundamentally different from similar restrictions imposed in non-Fascist countries. *Laissez faire* as a comprehensive policy has never existed at all and is certainly not to be found in any of the modern industrialized nations. Italy and Germany nevertheless approach the question of government control over economic activities in a spirit entirely different from that of the democracies or of the Soviet Union, a spirit which bears the marks of that confused struggle between romanticism, metaphysics, and radicalism which is characteristic of the two régimes.

THE CORPORATE STATE

The Italian Corporate State has its roots in the past syndicalist history of the Italian labor movement and is built around that already familiar principle of Mussolini which denies that the class struggle is one of the necessary moving forces of progress, but admits the existence of the conflict between the interests of capital and labor. This tenet has been finally embodied in the Corporate State which provides for two parallel sets of institutions: the associations or syndicates of employers and of employees, with the State and Fascist Party as the supreme arbiter and connecting link. The principle itself was not accepted without a struggle. Some of the Fascist leaders, among them Edmondo Rossoni, were ardently in favor of the creation of a single organization in which employers and workers should both participate. To this proposal the Confederation of Italian Industries, an association of employers, took strong exception. The matter was finally settled in favor of maintaining the identity of both the employers' and the workers' organizations. In December 1923 the decision was embodied in the so-called agreement of the Palazzo Chigi which was itself the outcome of a meeting between the representatives of the associations of employers and of workers over which Mussolini presided. A further important step toward the creation of the Corporate State was the agreement of the Palazzo Vidoni on October 2, 1925, when the employers recognized the Fascist Confederation of Workers as the sole representative of labor, and the latter recognized the Confederation of Italian Industries as the sole representative of the employers. All relations between the two parties were to be carried on through the instrumentality of the two Confederations. Thus the road was cleared for the establishment of the Corporate State.

The Law of April 3, 1926, gave the association of the employers and that of the workers legal recognition and provided that no more than one such association should be so established for each category of production; that is, one for the employers and one for the workers. Such legal recognition is granted by a Royal Decree on three general conditions: that the association shall comprise not less than ten per cent of the total number of workers employed in that particular branch of production in a given locality; that the association make provision not only for the protection of the economic interests of its members, but also for the advancement of their social welfare, and their "patriotic and moral" education; and that the leaders of the associations "give guarantee of ability, morality and sound national loyalty." The association which secures legal recognition becomes the sole representative of the employers or workers, of the category concerned, for the territorial subdivision covered by the association, irrespective of whether such employees or workers are members of the association or not. Other professional associations are not prohibited, but their sphere of action is so limited by the powers of the legally recognized associations that the high-sounding declaration of the Charter of Labor that "there is complete freedom of professional or syndicalist organizations" remains a dead letter.

The local associations of employers and workers which are organized on the occupational principle, form the basis of the pyramid which comprises communal, provincial and inter-provincial associations, then federations and, at the top, the national confederations. The number of the latter, since 1934, has been reduced to nine. There is one national confederation of employers and one national confederation of workers for each of the four chief fields of economic activity: industry, agriculture, commerce, and banking and insurance. The ninth national confederation consists of organizations of artists and members of the liberal professions.[1]

The principal object of the associations of employers and workers in the early days was the settlement of labor disputes, the conclusion of collective labor contracts, and also educational and social work. These functions they have retained ever since. But even then the Law of April 3, 1925, mentions as among the purposes of the associations "measures for promoting and improving national production." The Law of July 1, 1926, speaks of the corporation as a liaison organ of the "national syndical organizations of the several factors of production." It is there described as "an organ of State administration" and it has among its functions that of "promoting, encouraging and subsidizing all initiative which is designed to coordinate and improve production." The Charter of Labor further develops the idea of the Corporate State. "Corporations," says Article 6 of the Charter, "constitute the unitary organization of all forces of production and integrally represent their interests. In virtue of this integral representation, since the interests of production are the interests of the Nation, the corporations are

---

[1] The Law of February 5, 1934, establishing the corporations, provides that the local associations below the grade of federation must be "autonomous." A decree of August 16, 1934, puts this provision into effect by revoking the legal recognition which such associations enjoyed in the past, their powers being now derived from the confederations. An exception is made of the associations of artists and professional men. This change of status does not affect the factual position of local associations which continue to remain the basis of the corporate system.

recognized by the law as State organs. Representing the unitary interests of production, corporations may enforce binding regulations for the discipline of labor relations as well as for the affiliated associations." Improvement of production is also the immediate object of the association of employers who, according to Article 8 of the Charter, "are required to promote by all possible means the increase and improvement of production and reduction of costs." And Article 9 provides that "State intervention in economic production enters in only when private initiative is lacking or insufficient, or when the political interests of the State are involved. This intervention may take the form of control, assistance or direct management." The Fascist State is primarily a State of "producers" and this is why even the confederation representing artists and liberal professions is requested by the Charter "to promote the interests of art, science and letters, with a view to improving production and to the achievement of the moral object of the syndicalist system"!

The corporations heralded by the Charter of Labor did not materialize until 1934. In the meantime the National Council of Corporations, which had existed since 1926 as a merely advisory body within the Ministry of Corporations, was reorganized on an entirely new basis by the Law of March 20, 1930. It became the first official link between the associations of employers and those of employees. Since

1930 the Head of the Government has presided over the Council, which consists of the members of the cabinet, high officials of the Fascist Party and representatives of the associations elected by the respective organizations and appointed by Royal Decree upon the proposal of the Head of the Government. The jurisdiction of the National Council is very broad. It includes the "application and integration of the principles of the Charter of Labor according to the development of the corporate system and the requirements of production." Moreover the Council "may be called upon to give its opinion on any question whatsoever relating to national production."

The last and crowning step toward the creation of the Corporate State was the Law of February 5, 1934, and the decrees that put its provisions into effect. Corporations which had for so long been promised now came into being as liaison organs between the associations of employers and of workers. Mussolini defined them as "instruments which, under the aegis of the State, carry out the integral, organic and unitary discipline of productive forces, with a view to the development of the wealth, the political power and the welfare of the Italian people." In less abstract terms a corporation may be said to be a group of industrial, professional and trade associations united under a board known as the council of the corporation. The selection of the associations and syndicates which are included in each corporation is based on the idea of the "cycle of production." That is, it embraces all the phases of a process of production from the getting together of the raw materials to the sale of the finished goods. In certain cases the inter-connected cycles of production have been brought together into the same corporation. The council of the corporation is headed by a member of the cabinet, an under-secretary of State, or the Secretary of the Fascist Party. The members of the councils of corporations are elected by the affiliated organizations and are appointed by the Head of the Government on the recommendation of the Minister of Corporations. In 1935 the two offices were held by Mussolini. Each council includes technical experts and representatives of the State and the Fascist Party who, according to Mussolini, watch over the interests of the consumers. The membership of the councils varies from 67, in the case of the Corporation of the Chemical Industry, to 15 for the Corporation of Beet and Sugar. The total number of members of the councils of corporations in 1935 was 823, of which 318 represented employers, 315 labor, 34 technical experts, 19 artisans, 11 cooperative organizations, 19 public institutions, 41 liberal professions and artists, and 66 the Fascist Party.

The number of corporations in 1935 was 22. They were subdivided, according to the "cycle of production" into three classes: (1) corporations connected with agriculture, industry and commerce; (2) corporations connected with industry and commerce;

and (3) corporations connected with services.[2] The field of activity of the corporations is very broad and includes, in addition to the duties specified in the Charter of Labor and subsequent legislation already mentioned, that of "regulating economic relations and the unitary discipline of production." The decisions of the corporations were originally subject to the approval of the National Council of Corporations and became law if and when promulgated by a decree of the Head of the Government. By the Law of April 18, 1935, the first of these provisions was changed in the sense that the decisions of the corporations are now approved not by the National Council of Corporations, which is a large assembly, but by the Central Corporative Committee, a much smaller body, consisting of members of the Cabinet, the Secretary of the Fascist Party, the vice-presidents of the 22 corporations, presidents of the national confederations of employers and of workers, and representatives of other organizations.

THE CORPORATE STATE IN ACTION

This very bare outline of corporate structure will perhaps suffice to bring out its extraordinary complexity. The elements of duplication and overlap-

[2] The complete list is as follows: cereals, fruits, vegetables and flowers; viticulture and wine; beet and sugar; edible oil; animal husbandry and fisheries; forestry, lumber and wood; textiles and engineering; chemicals, clothing; paper and publishing; building, water, gas, and electricity; mining and quarrying; glass and pottery; credit and insurance; arts and professions; sea and air transportation; inland communications; public entertainment; hospitality.

ping are many. The basic units—the associations of employers and of workers—are organized on the vertical principle into national confederations, and on the horizontal principle into corporations. They also send their representatives to the provincial councils of corporate economy which were established in 1931 and are officially described as "corporations on a provincial scale." There seem to be at least two "corporate Parliaments": the National Council of Corporations and the Chamber of Deputies which consists very largely, it will be remembered, of members selected from the lists sent to the Grand Council of Fascism by the national confederations of employers and of workers. No wonder the abolition of the Chamber of Deputies is generally anticipated. The councils of the 22 corporations were moreover convened by the Duce in a joint session in the autumn of 1934. This looked suspiciously like a third corporate Parliament! There are also the Central Corporative Committee, the Ministry of Corporations, the Senate, and the Grand Council of Fascism, all of which possess rather broad if somewhat indeterminate powers in the shaping of the institutions and policies of the Corporate State. And last but not least there are the ubiquitous Fascist Party and the *Capo del Governo* himself whose consent is required and whose powers are unlimited. In theory the officers of the associations are elected, but in practice only men acceptable to the Government and the Party are nominated. The associations of the various grades are under the close supervision of the ministers, the prefects or the communal authorities. These officials exercise the right of veto over the appointment of the officers of the associations. I was assured at the Ministry of Corporations that no instance of the use of this right of veto is on record. It is the duty of the Fascist Party to see to it that no undesirable person can ever be nominated.

What is the real purpose of this elaborate structure? "The corporation is formed to increase the wealth, the political power, and the well-being of the Italian people," according to Mussolini. "These three objectives are conditional each on the other. Political strength creates wealth, and wealth in its turn invigorates political action. I should like to call your attention to the objective stated: the well-being of the Italian people. It is essential that these institutions we have set up may at a given moment be felt by the masses themselves as instruments through which those masses improve their standard of living." This purpose, which is commendable, is to be achieved, in the words of the Duce, "through the self-discipline of the categories concerned."

The element of free cooperation and self-discipline is always emphasized in Fascist theory, but is it carried into practice in Fascist institutions? The powers of the elaborate system of corporate bodies are merely advisory and the institutions themselves are under the complete control of the Party. The bringing of a very large percentage of the employers and workers [3] into closely knit and well-regimented trade associations may be of considerable help in carrying into effect various measures for the coordination of industrial production. Such associations may certainly tender useful advice to the Government in dealing with technical problems. But this is hardly a sufficient justification for Mussolini's statement that "Corporativism supersedes Socialism and supersedes liberalism: it creates a new synthesis." What Mussolini presumably means is that the corporate system supersedes Socialism because it is based, in theory, on the voluntary cooperation of the producers of every stage. This, as we have seen, is not the case in practice, since only one association for each category is legally recognized, its decisions are binding on all those employed in that trade whether they are members of the association or not, and the organization itself is under the complete control of the Government and the Fascist Party. Mussolini's second claim for coporativism—that it supersedes liberalism—seems to reflect the belief that the organization of branches of production into professional associations is something alien to economic liberalism. Such associations nevertheless exist in the non-Fascist countries whose doom has been so often sounded by the Duce. There is no question that the

[3] On December 31, 1934, the membership of the associations of employees was 1.5 million, representing 7.8 million people; and the membership of the associations of workers was 4.7 million, representing 7.1 million people.

Government and the Fascist Party have built up a powerful machinery for the control of the economic activities of the Nation, and that they have in their hands an instrument which is more obedient than that at the disposal of mere democracies. But it is extremely difficult to say whether it is really more effective. It is readily admitted that under the Fascist rule Italy has made considerable progress along the road of industrialization and the development of her national resources. But it is by no means clear that this was due to the "self-discipline of the categories concerned," as claimed by the Duce, and not perhaps to the influence of his own dynamic personality, vastly amplified through the machinery of the Party. The State and the Party are so closely associated with the work of the corporate institutions and play so important a part in their decisions that it would be idle to attempt to discover which decisions are the result of official pressure and which are due to self-discipline.

The early resolutions of the new corporations offer little guidance as to their future course. The corporations which met in the first eight months of 1935 concerned themselves largely with technical problems of the respective trades, with special emphasis on the development of those branches of production which could result in the reduction of imports from abroad. Such measures were taken, for instance, in the case of flax, wool, alcohol distilled from beets, and lubricating oil. In dealing with these matters the corporations, which are representative organizations of the trades concerned, can naturally be of great assistance to the Government in carrying out its policies.

The right of private property and individual enterprise has not been seriously curtailed by the corporate organization. Nevertheless some minor legislative restrictions have been introduced. The Decree of June 16, 1932, for instance, provided for the compulsory membership of enterprises in an association (*consortium*) if and when the Head of the Government so orders. This measure, like a number of others which have been decided upon since the beginning of the depression, is directed toward the strengthening of the industrial structure, which was showing signs of great weakness. The Government also took a prominent part in rescuing the banks; and it aided in the reorganization of industrial enterprises by creating first the *Istituto Mobiliare Italiano,* at the end of 1931 and then, about a year later, the *Istituto per la Ricostruzione Industriale.* The business of the latter institution is the refinancing of industrial enterprises and the liquidation of those that are no longer sound. These steps, however, like those for the control of foreign trade and the promotion of substitutes for commodities imported from abroad, must be considered as measures of expediency rather than as an integral part of the policy of the Corporate State. The Law of January 12, 1933, which requires a government license for the installment of new industrial plants or the extension of the existing ones, is in a different class. It is in harmony with the Fascist idea of the duty of the State to direct private initiative into the channels where it will best serve the interests of the community. The practical effect of this measure has so far been slight.

Until the beginning of the East African campaign there had been no attempt to control prices by legislative measures, although the level of prices had been influenced by Government intervention and also by pressure from the Party. In relatively few cases have the volume and nature of production been affected by the activities of the corporate bodies. There have been instances, although I was told exceptional ones, of the cutting down of the high salaries of officers of industrial enterprises and banks, but such action came not from the corporate institutions but from the Government. More significant are the changes that have taken place in the relations between employers and labor; they will be discussed in the next chapter. Yet, although the position of the private enterprise has not been directly impaired, the tying up of the economic organization of the country with its political machine and with the machine of the Party has introduced a degree of State control that opens practically boundless possibilities for further expansion of government intervention. Viewed from this angle, the end of economic liberalism announced by Mussolini is a great deal more than an empty phrase. It would seem however to be the result not so much of the growth of the "corporate spirit" which the Fascist organization is supposed to promote, as of the direct and indirect action of the State and the Party.

THE GERMAN VERSION

The economic program of the National Socialist Party, as has already been pointed out, offered practically unlimited latitude for interpretation. The Hitler movement has grown with such fantastic speed and has carried in its fold so many different elements whose economic and social aspirations were anything but identical that it would have been unreasonable to expect the Government of January 1933 to produce a coherent scheme of economic reorganization. The first months of the National Socialist régime were largely devoted to political reforms and to the consolidation of its power. There was much talk of the creation of a Corporate State which would combine some of the features of the Italian organization with those of the German medieval guilds. A definite step in this direction was the organization, on September 13, 1933, of the "Agricultural Estate" (*Reichsnährstand*) which proved an effective method of bringing the entire agriculture and food industry under the control of the Government.[4] A few days later, on September 22, 1933, the Reich Chamber of Culture (*Reichskulturkammer*) came into being. It was put under the control of the Ministry of Propaganda of which Dr. Goebbels is

[4] See below, p. 179 *sqq.*

Augsburg Seminary
Library

the head, and extended its jurisdiction and supervision to art, music, literature, the press, the theater and the radio, the moving picture industry and advertising. The last was led to organize itself in a special council under the Reich Chamber of Culture and was made subject to a very close and detailed government control. But the bulk of German industry was not subjected to regimentation until the end of 1934, although in the meantime the hand of the State gradually made itself felt.

On February 27, 1934, came the "Law for the Organic Reconstruction of German Business" (*Gesetz zur Vorbereitung des organischen Aufbaus der deutschen Wirtschaft*) which conferred upon the Minister of Economics wide powers. The Minister was authorized to name trade associations as sole representatives of any branch of commerce or industry; to make membership in such associations obligatory for all firms engaged in that line of business; and also to set up new trade associations and merge or dissolve the existing ones. This decree introduced into business organization the principle of leadership, which is an essential element in the National Socialist ideology. By virtue of these powers the Minister of Economics issued a decree on March 13, 1934, by which all the industrial and commercial activities of the country, except those included in the Agricultural Estate and in the Reich Chamber of Culture, were organized into 12 *Hauptgruppen*. Seven of them comprised the chief industries, and the remaining five included handicrafts, commerce,

banks and credit, insurance and transport. A thirteenth *Hauptgruppe*, that of public utilities (*Energie-
wirtschaft*) was soon added. All the numerous
trade associations that existed in Germany in the
past were brought under the sway of the new organization. This coordination of industrial and commercial associations did not seem greatly to alter the
situation and had little effect except, perhaps, in so
far as they minimized their cost to members by a
certain reduction of overlapping charges.

On August 2, 1934, Dr. Hjalmar Schacht succeeded Dr. Kurt Schmitt as Minister of Economics,
and the reorganization of business entered upon a
new phase. A decree of November 27, 1934, established the Reich Chamber of Economics (*Reichswirtschaftskammer*) the constitution of which was
further developed and elaborated by the Decree of
May 3, 1935. The business organization that grew
out of this legislation is one of extraordinary complexity. The semi-official diagram depicting the new
structure has driven to despair not only foreign students but also many of the German officials who,
presumably, are fully conversant with the intricacies
of the German way of thinking. Reduced to its
fundamental elements the Reich Chamber of Economics may be said to consist of two sets of organizations: (1) the *Reichsgruppen* (industry,[5] commerce,
banks, insurance, public utilities, and handicrafts)
which, with their local organs, are professional asso-

---

[5] The *Reichsgruppe Industrie* is subdivided into seven *Hauptgruppen* embracing various branches of industry.

ciations of the respective branches of economic activity organized on the vertical principle; and (2)
the chambers of commerce and industry, which are
regional associations organized on the territorial or
horizontal principle. The distinction between the
two sets of organizations as vertical and horizontal
is not absolutely correct but it gives a fair picture
of the principle underlying the whole structure. The
same industrial and commercial enterprises therefore
are controlled by the Reich Chamber of Economics
for different purposes, either through the *Reichsgruppen* or through the Federation of the Chambers
of Commerce and Industry. For the chambers of
commerce and industry are organized into a Federation (*Arbeitsgemeinschaft der Industrie- und Han-
delskammern in der Reichswirtschaftskammer*) which
is incorporated in the Reich Chamber of Economics.
The conservative and old-established chambers of
commerce and industry, the complete abolition of
which was freely predicted, not only survived the
reorganization but retained their identity and are
even represented in the Reich Chamber of Economics as a separate unit through their Federation. This
has provoked much comment and has been interpreted by many as a victory for the conservative elements. It is impossible to say to what extent this
interpretation is correct, although there is little
doubt that the maintenance of the chambers of commerce and industry did not displease business.

The unquestionable result of the creation of the
Chamber of Economics has been that the Govern-

ment now has practically unlimited power over the entire business of the country and unlimited possibilities for influencing it. The Chamber of Economics, like all National Socialist institutions, is based on the leadership principle. Its president, as also the president of the Federation of the Chambers of Commerce and Industry, is appointed by the Minister of Economics; and all other officials of the organization and of its local ramifications are appointed from above, and not elected as they were formerly in the old trade associations. The budget of the Chamber of Economics is, moreover, subject to approval by the Minister of Economics. The purpose of the reorganization as it emerges from official and semi-official comments is both to increase the hold of the State over business and likewise fundamentally to change the character of professional and trade associations. The duties of the appointed leaders of German business are rather to promote "national solidarity" (*Gemeinschaft*) than to defend professional or trade interests. It is presumed that the Chamber of Economics will outgrow the traditional professional and class mentality which its component parts may possibly still retain from former days and develop into an institution guided primarily by national interests. This is the familiar principle of the National Socialist program: *Gemeinnutz vor Eigennutz*. Perhaps not all German business men are enthusiastic about it, but they keep quiet. Incidentally, one of the minor purposes of the reorganization was the desire to reduce, by eliminating overlapping, the cost to business of the maintenance of the trade associations. Judging by reports that have appeared in the German press this object of the Chamber of Economics was not achieved in the first months of its operation. It would seem that in a number of cases the cost to business has increased and not diminished.

The most remarkable feature of the German organization of business is, perhaps, the peculiar position in which the employers find themselves toward labor. Here the difference between the Fascist and the National Socialist approach comes out clearly. Fascism, it will be remembered, believes in the existence of a conflict between capital and labor and has built up the Corporate State around two parallel sets of organizations, one for the employers and one for labor. But they are kept separate. Only in the councils of the corporations and other bodies and under the auspices of the State and the Party do they meet on a footing of equality. But Germany's National Socialism denies the existence of any conflict of interests between capital and labor and has carried this principle into practice. The Law of January 20, 1934, for the Organization of National Labor declared that the owner of an enterprise was its leader, and that his employees were his followers (*Gefolgschaft*), and that they all "worked together for the furtherance of the purposes of the enterprise, and for the benefit of the Nation and the State in General." It has already been pointed out that in accordance with the National Socialist theory the

employer is not a "hereditary enemy" of labor, but
merely a coworker in the common enterprise. The
employers were accordingly induced to join the Labor Front (*Arbeitsfront*),[6] an organization that came
into existence in the early summer of 1933 and absorbed the former trade unions. This, however, was
not deemed sufficient. On March 26, 1935, Dr.
Schacht, the Minister of Economics, entered into an
agreement with Dr. Robert Ley, the leader of the
Labor Front, by virtue of which the Reich Chamber
of Economics as a body joined the Labor Front. The
members of associations represented in the Chamber
of Economics, therefore, became members of the Labor Front in a double capacity: individually, as
leaders of industrial enterprises, and again, collectively—through the Chamber of Economics—which
seems rather absurd. But, in addition to this metaphysical aspect the agreement also had certain very
definite and important provisions. The Chamber of
Economics became the Economic Department (*Wirt-
schaftsamt*) of the Labor Front, which would seem
to mean that no economic measures of any importance can be taken by the Labor Front and its leader
without the advice of the Chamber, which is subordinated to the Minister of Economics, Dr. Schacht.
There can, for instance, be no increase in wages
without his approval. As a connecting link between
the Chamber of Economics and the Labor Front a
special Labor and Economic Board (*Reichsarbeits-
und Wirtschaftsrat*) came into existence. It is com-

[6] See below, p. 136 *sqq.*

posed of the higher officials of the two organizations, with the participation of the Minister of Economics and the Leader of the Labor Front. The purpose of the new Board is to cooperate with the Government, the Chamber of Economics and the Labor Front in deciding questions of economic and social policy.

The agreement of March 26 was regarded by Dr. Ley as a great victory for labor and by all the official commentators in general as a striking manifestation of that national unity which overshadows almost all other preoccupations in the German mind today. Dr. Schacht celebrated the occasion by delivering an eloquent speech on the same subject. Appropriately, he addressed his audience as *"Meine deutschen Volksgenossen, liebe Arbeitskameraden."* But the unofficial comments in certain quarters would seem to indicate that the victory of Dr. Ley was not quite so complete as he professed to believe it, and that the position of business has been strengthened rather than weakened by the agreement of March 26. A distinguished German industrialist to whom I remarked that a double membership in the Labor Front would seem somewhat superfluous and that by joining it as individuals and again collectively German business was "more labor than labor itself" (*plus royaliste que le roi*), adjusted his monocle, sighed, and said that Germany was living through a revolution that was not merely national but also social; that the psychological effect of business joining the Labor Front was enormous; and that at the same time the interests of business were safeguarded by Dr. Schacht's control over the economic activities of the Labor Front. It may be doubted whether this is a real safeguard. What matters in Germany today is the attitude of the Chancellor and the Party. It is only as an interpretation of this attitude that the changes in the organization of business acquire their real meaning.

STATE INTERVENTION

In Germany more than in Italy the rights of private property and individual initiative have been subjected to rather important limitations. By the Law for the Organization of National Labor, enacted on January 20, 1934, the owner of a business may be removed if he "abuses his authority . . . by maliciously exploiting the labor of any of his followers (employees) or wounding their sense of honor." Instances of the removal of owners, I was assured, are rare but have nevertheless occurred, usually on the ground of "anti-social" conduct. For example, a baker in the Rhineland had trouble with his employees. His establishment was inspected and declared unsanitary. The owner was removed and replaced by a trustee appointed by local authorities. The salary of the trustee was paid from the profits of the enterprise and the owner was entitled to whatever was left. Such removals have also taken place on political grounds. No definite information as to the number of cases is available, but I was told that they represent merely a fraction of one per cent.

Nevertheless the very possibility of such action exercises a strong pressure to prevent "anti-social" conduct.

Another example. A foreign government invited bids for the building of a munitions factory. The German Government, which has invested large sums in the heavy industries, instructed the eligible firms not to submit bids below a certain figure. One of the firms disregarded this ruling and tendered a bid that was under the minimum set. The head of the firm was ordered to appear before a tribunal that consisted of the members of the *Reichsgruppe*. His conduct was censured. He was permitted to continue in office but was warned that in case of any further disregard of official instructions his firm would be excluded from participation in government orders, which are considerable, and that he might be removed altogether. The threat of exclusion from government orders is usually sufficient to keep every one in line. The "trial" was a purely administrative measure and had no basis in law.

The Law of July 15, 1933, gave the Minister of Economics the power to prevent the extension of the existing industrial plants, to revise cartel agreements already made, and to force individual firms to enter into cartels or other industrial combinations. The purpose of this legislation was to maintain a stable level of prices. A number of the suggested cartels were organized, for instance, those for glassware, newsprint, nails and springs, and other manufactures. Some compulsory cartels were set up for only a short time to afford the industries concerned opportunities to reach voluntary agreements. In many instances the threat of compulsory cartelization proved sufficient to prevent "unfair" competition and underselling. And the Minister also made free use of his power to prevent further expansion of industrial plants when, in his opinion, the existing capacity was adequate to meet the demand. No business expansion was permitted without a government license. At the beginning these prohibitions applied to old-established industries. Later on, however, they were used in case of new industries on the ground that it was the duty of the Government to prevent mal-investment of capital. A large number of industries were affected by this policy, among them manufactures of textiles, electric cables, paper, radio receivers, rubber tires, cigarettes and many other things. In the case of the textile industry the prohibition on expansion was accompanied by a limitation of working hours to 36 a week, a measure designed to further the spread of employment. The Decree of July 16, 1934, prohibited the starting of machinery that had not been running for four weeks, unless it was accompanied by the stopping of machinery of equal capacity.

Department stores, it will be remembered, were among the institutions the abolition of which National Socialism had advocated as early as 1920. In 1931 their trade represented about 10 per cent of the entire retail output of the country, and that of the cooperative stores, about 5 per cent. National

Socialism had always proclaimed its intention of defending the small traders against the competition of these large concerns which, moreover, were mainly in Jewish hands. The complete liquidation of department stores, however, proved more difficult than was anticipated; for it became evident that it would inevitably lead to unemployment and the fight against that condition came first in the policy of the Hitler Government. The one-price and chain stores were also extremely unpopular with the National Socialists. By the Law of May 10, 1933, the opening of more such concerns was altogether prohibited, thus making permanent a measure enacted by a decree of the von Schleicher Government which forbade the same thing for a period of 15 months. The Law of May 12, 1933, extended the prohibition to all retail establishments on the ground that they were already too numerous. In this case the prohibition was to last for only six months. But subsequent legislation and the Law of September 13, 1934, made the general measure permanent. No retail shop could be opened without a license. The issuance of such licenses was made dependent not only on the need of a new shop in the locality in question but also on the standing of the applicant, who must prove that he was properly qualified to enter the trade. In this way "undesirable elements" were to be completely excluded from retail trade since the requirement of a proper qualification applied both to the opening of new establishments and likewise to the sale of those already in operation.

The entire advertising business, as was indicated above, has, since the autumn of 1933, been under the strict supervision of the Advertising Council and the Ministry of Propaganda, and is subject to licensing on the ground of personal qualifications.

A rather important restriction on the freedom of employers of labor was introduced in August 1934 in connection with the unemployment program. Most of the employees under twenty-five years of age were to be dismissed and replaced by older people. Skilled workers and some who were married were exempted from the application of this measure. The dismissed workers were encouraged by various means to seek employment in agriculture.

More significant was the Bank Reform Law of December 5, 1934. Since the banking crisis of 1931 the German Government has been exercising a wide control over the entire banking system of the country. It was the intervention of the State that saved German banking from complete collapse in 1931 and it left the Government with a controlling or a substantial minority interest in four of the five largest banks. In 1933 a Bank Investigation Committee was set up to determine the causes of the recent banking crisis. Its report, which was published in November 1934 was looked forward to with much apprehension in financial circles. There was great relief, therefore, when the Committee declared itself against nationalization but in favor of a strict supervision of the banking system. The Bank Reform Law of December 5, 1934, reaffirmed the provision of an earlier law which prohibited the opening of new credit institutions or new branches, and made them subject to license. The granting of a license, as in the case of retail trade, depended not only on the financial standing, but also on the business and moral qualifications of the applicant. The Law also provided for the establishment of a Bank Supervision Board (*Aufsichtsamt für das Kreditwesen*) which has very wide powers in dealing with the banking situation. The Board consists of the President of the Reichsbank, a representative of the Chancellor, and some of the higher government officials. One of its chief objects is to keep the banks in a liquid condition and to bring their policy into line with that of the Government. The Board of the Reichsbank, which used to elect its President, was abolished, and the President of the Reichsbank will now be nominated by the Chancellor.

The right of German corporations to pay dividends was limited by the Law of March 29, 1934; this law, in turn, was made more drastic by the Law on Dividend Investment enacted December 4, 1934. In accordance with the latter legislation, the dividends payable to shareholders may not be greater than 6 per cent or, in certain cases, 8 per cent. If earnings rise above this figure the corporation must turn them over to the *Golddiskontbank*, which acts as a trustee for the shareholders and invests the surplus dividends in government loans for a period of three years. The sum so "loaned" will be turned over to the shareholders then. The reason for such legislation is the desire of the Government to strengthen its credit and to increase the funds at its disposal for fighting unemployment. The measure is moreover justified on the ground that the increased earnings of the corporations are not infrequently due to large government orders and to the investment of public funds.

BUSINESS IN THE TOTALITARIAN STATE

It will appear from the above survey that industry, commerce, banking and other fields of economic activity, both in Italy and in Germany, have been subjected to a very advanced degree of government regimentation. It will be seen later that the hand of the State has made itself felt even more strongly in agriculture. We shall also have to review the truly formidable array of prohibitions and restrictions which have descended upon the business organizations of the two countries as a result of the decline of their international trade, coupled with exchange difficulties. It may be said in anticipation that such restrictive policies cannot be held to form an integral part of the program of the totalitarian State, but are dictated by considerations of expedience or, to be more exact, of dire necessity. On the other hand, the coordination of business activities, which took the form of the Corporate State in Italy and of the Chamber of Economics in Germany, where it has a peculiar relationship to the Labor Front, is unquestionably an attempt to carry into effect the principles which the two movements are preaching. I have already pointed out that there are important and significant differences between the Italian and the German structures. Although Hitler has been in power for a much shorter period than has Mussolini the German methods of control and State intervention are probably more far-reaching and rigid than they are in Italy. But if there are differences, there are also important likenesses which may be considered as typical of the character of the totalitarian State.

A distinguished German official, with whom I was discussing the Chamber of Economics, explained to me that the whole structure of business control was really patterned after the army. It was built up around the principles of hierarchy, unity of command and strict discipline which were expected eventually to produce that *esprit de corps* or common will which Mussolini calls "corporate spirit." The Italian Corporate State has a very similar foundation; and although it does not recognize the leadership principle of National Socialism, it believes in hierarchy, the rule of the *élite* and unity of command. And for all practical purposes the difference between the appointed officials of today's Germany and the "elected" officials of today's Italy is very slight indeed.

But this common will or corporate spirit which is to guide the institutions of the totalitarian State is something still to come. The whole organization depends at the present entirely on the Party, which is just as much the mainstay of the economic system as it is the pillar of the political régime. A movement which draws its ideology from the glorification of free cooperation and preaches the sacrifice of individual interests to those of the community maintains itself in power by methods that have little to do with its own theories. Whatever may happen to the Italian Corporate State and to its German counterpart in the future, if and when the coming generations develop the corporate spirit or assimilate the ideas of *Gemeinschaft,* at present conditions are far from ideal. Bureaucracy is abhorrent to Fascism and National Socialism, just as it is abhorrent to Russian Communism. In spite of that fact, however, it must be admitted that Italy and Germany have developed huge bureaucratic machines which may well be compared with that of the Soviet Union. There would seem to be a government bureau in every house in Berlin's Tiergarten district, and in every second palazzo in Rome. The whole structure, as I have pointed out, is cumbersome and awkward in the extreme. It is true, however, that in this respect democracies can also make comparisons and have little to learn from dictatorships. Witness the luxuriant growth of bureaus and departments in the United States under the New Deal. The tortuous bureaucratic methods of Fascism and National Socialism are much resented by the business community. The head of an Italian exporting firm, who was a member of the Fascist Party, described the interminable complications that surround the issue of an export license—even before the Ethiopian campaign—and added mournfully: "Now on top of all these are to come the corporations," which did not augur well for the "corporate spirit." And a German official with whom I was exploring the terrifying chart depicting the ramifications of the Reich Chamber of Economics, said apologetically: "We are living through an orgy of organization." Strange things can happen to the spirit of free cooperation for the common good when it gets caught in the cogs of a powerful political organization.

CHAPTER V

THE END OF CLASS STRUGGLE

THE BASIC PRINCIPLES

The approach of Fascism and National Socialism to the labor question is all the more interesting since it attempts to solve a problem that every advanced country, whatever its political complexion, has to face. It brings out, moreover, and in high relief, the perplexing variety of elements that enter into the ideology of the two movements. The Italian Charter of Labor declares that "work in all its forms—intellectual, technical and manual—both organizing and executive is a social duty." The program of the National Socialist Party, which preceded the Charter by some seven years, is just as emphatic. "The first duty of every citizen, says Article 10 of the program, "is to work either with brain or with hand." This sounds dangerously like the well-known Communist slogan: "He who does not work, does not eat." There is, however, no reason to be unduly alarmed because, as we know, Mussolini and Hitler quite as definitely deny the reality of the class struggle, the second fundamental principle of Communism, as they uphold the duty to work. The Italian and German solution of the labor problem consists in trying to build up a relationship between employers and em-

118

ployees which will eliminate once and for all the use of violent or "direct" methods in the settlement of labor disputes. The document, which embodies the principles of the Italian organization for the establishment of everlasting peace in the field of labor relations, is the Charter of Labor, of which Mussolini was the author. Although, when issued in 1927, it was merely a party document it has since been given legal recognition by the Italian courts. The German counterpart of the Charter of Labor is the Law for the Organization of National Labor, enacted January 20, 1934. In the present records of the respective countries these two acts occupy a place of honor akin to that of the Bible in Christian communities, Magna Charta in England, and the Constitution in the United States. While the German Law of January 30, 1934, is relatively little known abroad, the fame of the Charter of Labor has long since spread over the frontiers of Italy and has attracted much attention, not always unsympathetic even in quarters where Fascism, as a whole, is not altogether popular. As happens only too often, a close examination of the famous document adds but little to its glamor.

INDUSTRIAL RELATIONS IN ITALY

Strictly speaking, the Charter of Labor is not really the Magna Charta of Italian labor, but rather the key link in a chain of legislation. Parts of it had already been enacted and additions were made later,

This legislation laid down definite rules for the organization of employers and workers in associations or syndicates, made compulsory the conclusion of collective labor contracts, prohibited strikes and lockouts, and for them substituted Labor Courts. This system has its basis in the organization of employers and workers in two separate groups of professional associations.[1] It is only the legally recognized associations that are permitted to represent the employers or workers of a given category in any particular district and to conclude labor contracts. They act also for those workers and employers who are not members of the association. These provisions, together with the rules governing the organization of associations, proved to be an effective means of bringing the entire labor movement under the close control of the Fascist Government and the Fascist Party. It will be remembered that the representation in an association of only 10 per cent of the entire number of people engaged in any professional pursuit is sufficient to enable it to obtain legal recognition, provided that the officers of the association are in good standing with the Government, and also that the "presidents" of the employers and the "secretaries" of the workers' associations have been elected by their fellow members and confirmed in their offices by the Government. The broad and exclusive powers of the legally recognized associations have made perfectly illusory the high-sounding pronouncement of the Charter of Labor upon the com-

[1] See above, p. 86 *sqq.*

plete freedom of the syndicalist movement. And the confirmation of their officers by the Government made equally illusory that freedom of election of their officers which, legally, the associations enjoy. The result has been that the Italian labor movement, albeit it has behind it a long and troubled history and a strong revolutionary tradition, has been driven into the straitjacket of Fascist controlled syndicates. This was undoubtedly a most important step toward the consolidation of the Fascist dictatorship. Modern factories and plants, with their large aggregations of men and women workers who often have good reason for discontent with the existing social and economic order, are a potential revolutionary factor which no absolutist régime can afford to disregard. Mussolini had been long and closely connected with the Italian labor movement and knew well the revolutionary potentialities of syndicalism. The gathering of the workers' syndicates into the fold of Fascism was therefore a decisive victory and it made possible further experiments in labor legislation.

The chief purpose of the entire complex system of corporate agencies set up in Italy is to eliminate labor disputes by subordinating the interests of the workers and the employers to the higher interests of the State and of the Nation. An important instrument for accomplishing this aim is the collective labor contract which is entered into by the associations of employers and of workers and is compulsory for all employers and workers of any given category.

The most troublesome question in the relations between the employers and the workers is naturally the question of wages. The Charter of Labor, with that lack of precision which is so characteristic of Fascist legislation, declares that "wages shall be determined not by any general rules but by agreement between the respective parties to the collective contract." If, however, there should be a disagreement as to wages, it shall be brought up first for conciliation before the associations and then, conciliation failing, for decision before the labor court. The court "will guarantee that wages shall correspond with the normal demands of life, with the possibilities of production, and the output of labor." In his illuminating and exhaustive study of the labor policies of the Fascist régime a distinguished French writer, M. L. Rosenstock-Franck, has made clear how superficial and shallow is this statement which cannot and does not give any real guidance to the labor courts. How is the court to determine what are the "normal demands of life" of the workers, what are "the possibilities of production," and what is the "output of labor?" And how is it to reach an equitable decision? To none of these all-important questions do the Labor Charter, subsequent legislation, or any decision of the courts themselves give an answer. The courts would seem to be guided merely by expediency, the exigencies of the political situation and the pressure brought upon them by the Government and the Party.

It is claimed that, in order to be effective, a collective contract must be comprehensive, that is, it must apply to all the workers engaged in any particular pursuit; that it must cover every essential element in the relations between employers and workers; and that it must be stable, i.e., it must give assurance of a certain permanency in the existing relations between the two parties. In Italy the first of these requirements is achieved, to repeat, through the powers that the legally recognized associations possess to enter into contracts binding on all employers and workers in any given category. The serious drawback of such an arrangement is that it makes it necessary to base the scale of wages on the output of the enterprises that are the least efficient, with consequences particularly unfavorable to the interests of the workers in the case of contracts effective on a national scale. It is true, however, that the conclusion of collective contracts does not preclude the conclusion of private agreements between employers and workers, provided that the stipulations of such agreements are not less favorable to labor than those of the collective contract. Italian legislation lays down definite rules as to the contents of labor contracts. Some of them present welcome innovations and are distinctly favorable to labor. In addition to provisions relating to wages, methods of their payment, and hours of labor, each collective contract must determine the weekly holiday, annual vacations, the amount of relief to be given the worker in case of illness, the indemnity to be paid in case of his dismissal through no fault of his own, and the indemnity to be paid to his family in the event of his death. Every contract must be submitted for approval to the Prefect or the Ministry of Corporations and is not valid until it has been published. Any infringement of the provisions of the collective contract is punishable by a fine and the offender is liable for such damages as may result to the party injured.

The law also specifically provides that every collective contract must be concluded for a definite period of time and that its provisions must be observed until the expiration of its term, thus guaranteeing a certain stability in the relations between employers and workers. There is, however, a very important exception to this rule. According to Article 71 of the Law of July 1, 1926 "action for the formulation of new labor conditions is permitted even when a collective contract has been stipulated, and prior to the date of its expiration, provided a considerable change has occurred in the actual conditions since the date of execution." M. Rosenstock-Franck has assembled a number of instances of such revisions, which have been demanded and made sometimes only a few weeks after the conclusion of the collective contract. The "considerable change in actual conditions," on which these demands were based, was the result of the economic difficulties in which Italy found itself in the period following 1927, in consequence of the revaluation of the lira on what is now generally believed to have been too high a level and, after 1929, in a time of world-wide depression. The employers were naturally in a position to produce strong and convincing arguments in favor of the reduction of wages, which are a heavy item in their costs; and the general level of wages, already appallingly low, was reduced in some cases by as much as 20 or 25 per cent, or even more. According to M. Rosenstock-Franck real wages declined between 1927 and 1930 by from 15 to 20 per cent. Syndicalist discipline certainly deserves credit for the resignation with which these heavy cuts were accepted by labor. The Fascist press unanimously acclaimed the magnificent spirit of sacrifice made evident when Italian workers were willing to disregard their immediate interests and to put them below those of "national production."

All lockouts and strikes are prohibited by the Law of April 3, 1926. The same law defines a lockout as the closing of a plant "without justifiable motive, and for the sole purpose of obtaining from the employees a revision in the existing labor agreements." A strike is defined as an abandonment of work by three or more employees, "by preconceived agreement." Both these definitions leave ample room for interpretation in the courts. Direct action by labor being thus eliminated, the Italian legislation provides that all labor disputes must be settled by conciliation or by the labor courts. The element of conciliation is strongly stressed and no action can be brought before the court unless attempts at conciliation have first been made through the association or the Ministry of Corporations. The labor courts are attached to every district court of appeal and consist of three judges. The judges are assisted by two experts selected from a special list. These labor courts are described by official Fascist writers as courts of equity, and they have to be guided by the familiar principle of protecting above all the "superior interests of production." The jurisdiction of the courts extends to all labor disputes, both collective and individual, when the latter are the outcome of a collective contract. One of their important and thorny tasks is to determine the "actual conditions of labor," which really means wages, in the absence of a collective contract or when such a contract has been revised. I have already mentioned the extreme difficulties presented by this problem. M. Rosenstock-Franck is right, I think, when he maintains that the decisions of the labor courts are based on political considerations and have little to do with the intricate economic questions which affect wages, cost of production, and so on.

A word must be said about the employment offices. These offices are attached to the local syndicates of workers. Employers are under an obligation enforced by severe fines to hire workers only through the agency of the employment office. The unemployed are under a similar obligation to register with the local office. Employers must accept the workers who are sent to them by the employment offices, and preference is given to men who are members of the Fascist Party or of the Fascist syndicates.

The machinery for the settlement of labor disputes outlined above has worked fairly satisfactorily in the sense that strikes and lockouts have practically disappeared, which in itself is no mean achievement. The reason for this marked change from the conditions which prevailed before the passing of the legislation of 1926 and 1927 lies perhaps not so much in the perfection of the machinery itself as in the effectiveness of the control exercised by the Fascist Party over both employers and labor. They are represented in labor disputes by the presidents and secretaries of their respective associations who, though "elected," are also confirmed in office by the Government. The judges are appointees of the Government. The list of experts who assist the judges is carefully selected by Fascist controlled organizations and approved by the president of the court of appeal. Most of them are members of the Party and are bound by Party discipline. Decisions are put into effect by the associations under the supervision of presidents and secretaries who are Party members. This goes a long way to explain why labor accepts without much outside sign of discontent heavy cuts in wages, which would certainly lead to violent outbursts in a democratic country. This is what is called in Italy "Fascist discipline." One should not imagine, however, that the labor courts always take the side of the employers. Fascist radicalism is by no means dead, and many of the leaders of the movement, from Mussolini down, have long been ardent champions of labor. If the decisions on wages in recent years have largely gone against labor this has been in consequence of Italy's unfortunate economic position. But in not a few instances the courts have favored labor against employers, and, in particular, they have taken a very lenient view of minor strikes. The conclusion to be drawn would seem to be that labor disputes are decided in Italy not so much by applying principles of equity, as by those of the Fascist policy of the day. And, again, it is the powerful hold of the Fascist Party that makes possible the enforcement of the decisions of the courts.

LABOR UNDER FASCISM

"Since we have had the Charter of Labor," wrote, in 1927, Giuseppe Bottai, one of the most enthusiastic supporters of the Corporate State and at one time Minister of Corporations, "there have been no limits to the possibilities of increasing the material and moral well-being of the individual." The actual condition of the working masses for whose benefit the Labor Charter was devised would hardly justify this statement. But Fascist writers were never conspicuous for moderation in the use of superlatives.

In approaching the economic position of Italian labor two important considerations should be borne in mind. The first is that in Italy the economic level of the working classes has always been shockingly low; and the second, that the introduction of Fascist labor legislation coincided with the beginning of the depression which made itself felt in Italy earlier than in other countries as a consequence, to repeat, of the revaluation of the lira on too high a basis in 1927. For neither of these two factors can the Fascist Government be held responsible, although the revaluation of the lira was, of course, its own work. In any case, though a lower valuation of the lira in terms of foreign currencies would undoubtedly have helped Italian foreign trade, it could not have nullified the unhappy effects of world depression to any substantial degree.

Statistics of wages and indices of the cost of living must always be used with caution, and Italian statistics have sometimes been severely criticized. They make no secret, however, of the fact that the level of wages has remained extremely low. In 1930 the average hourly pay of an industrial worker was 2 lire and in 1934 had declined to 1.66 lire; [2] the indices of the cost of living for the same years were respectively 430 and 336 (January–June of 1914 = 100). The hourly wage of a male agricultural laborer in 1930 was 1.49 lire and of a female, 0.86 lire; in 1934, the figures had fallen to 1.13 and 0.66. The index of real wages of the same workers was 157 in 1920–1924, 149 in 1930 and 143 in 1934 (1913–1914 = 100). The actual reduction of wages was, however, larger than would be indicated by these figures, because the number of working hours also declined. In the autumn of 1934 Mussolini took energetic measures to reduce unemployment, which was assuming menacing proportions. Addressing the

[2] The parity of the lira to the depreciated dollar is 8.9 cents.

workers of Milan in October he promised them
that "social justice" would be the keynote of the
Thirteenth Year of Fascism (November 1934–October 1935). The fulfillment of this pledge took the
form of an agreement between the national confederations of employers and workers which provided
for the introduction of the 40-hour week in all
branches of industry. Overtime work was prohibited,
the employment of women and boys was to be limited to such work as they were specially qualified to
do; persons in receipt of pensions or retirement ben-
efits were to be superseded by unemployed workers
who had no incomes. The effect of this job-sharing
could not be other than to reduce still further an already meager wage. At the hourly rate of 1.66 lire
an industrial worker employed 40 hours a week
would earn 66.40 lire, or, at the gold parity of the
lira, about $6. The earnings of agricultural laborers,
as we have seen, are considerably lower, those of
women amounting to less than one-half of those of
a male industrial worker. To convert the wages of
Italian labor into dollars is not a sound procedure.
Nevertheless it helps to illustrate the undeniable and
well-known fact that the economic standards of
wage-earners are appallingly low. Fascism, so far,
has failed to remedy this situation.

In Italy unemployment never was a problem of
quite the same magnitude as in the United States,
England or Germany. It is, moreover, subject to
very strong seasonal fluctuations, declining in the
summer and rising sharply in the winter months. In

recent years unemployment has shown an alarming
tendency to increase, a phenomenon observable in
every country. From the low level of 193,000 in
June 1929 the number of registered unemployed had
risen to 1,229,000 in February 1933. In January 1934
there were 1,158,000. A work-sharing program on
which the Government embarked in October 1934
and a revival of industrial activities connected with
the East African expedition and the drafting of
many men resulted in a substantial decrease in the
number of the unemployed, although this reduction
proved to be less than might have been expected.
This is explained by the fact that many of the employers did not replace the drafted men. At the beginning of July 1935 the unemployment figure was
still as high as 638,000, which was considerable for
that time of year, and higher than the corresponding figure for 1931, although it was some 200,000
less than the figure for June 1934. There are probably also a number of unemployed who escape regis-
tration, but how many cannot be accurately determined.

Unemployment insurance, which was introduced
in 1919 and reorganized in December 1923, cannot
be considered as adequate. It is compulsory for industrial workers earning less than 800 lire a month,
but does not include agricultural laborers who number about 2,000,000. The amount paid to the unemployed is very small, and no provision is made for
dependents. Eligibility to draw unemployment insurance is likewise surrounded with many legal

restrictions which reduce considerably the number of the beneficiaries. The proportion of the unemployed who actually receive payments on account of unemployment insurance is estimated at something like 25 to 30 per cent of the total.

As a measure of unemployment relief the Government has embarked on an extensive program of public works which provides for land improvements, housing, electrification, road building and archæological excavations. In 1934, 86 million days of work were created, and employment was provided for a daily average of 289,000 workers. For the same year the Public Work Office appropriated over 1,000 million lire for public works undertaken by the State, and this sum did not include the amounts spent by independent offices—some of them also engaged in road building, land reclamation, and provincial and municipal enterprises—which were considerable. For a poor country such as Italy this represents a very great financial effort, although it will hardly impress an American reader used to the gigantic figures given out every day under the New Deal.

If Fascism has not succeeded so far in contributing to the improvement of the economic position of the worker it has been very active in social work. A Maternity and Child Welfare Organization was established in 1925. An Institute of Social Insurance helps the beneficiaries under the various social insurance systems to obtain the payments to which they are entitled, and endeavors to make the working of social insurance smoother and more equitable. Much has been done in the field of public health and sanitation where Italy has always been notoriously backward.

The most important and probably the most successful of the Fascist social ventures is the great organization for recreation and sports, the *Dopolavoro* ("After Work") which, at the beginning of 1935, had more than 2,000,000 members. It is open to all workers and employees. For a very small fee they are entitled to the benefit of all its cultural and recreational activities. There is a *Dopolavoro* group in every workshop, factory and public administration office in the country. In addition to facilities for sports and exercise, the *Dopolavoro* sponsors activities that are literary, musical or theatrical; it organizes excursions, maintains libraries and provides its members with tickets at greatly reduced rates for concerts, moving pictures and theatrical performances. The *Dopolavoro* also furnishes medical attendance at a mere fraction of the normal fees. No less active is the *Opera Balilla,* an organization which concerns itself with the young people and brings them up in the true spirit of Fascism. In 1934 it had some 4.3 million members. The *Balilla* maintains a wide network of summer colonies on the seashore and in the mountains, where practically every young Italian today gets a chance to spend a few weeks; and this cannot but be beneficial to his body, whatever may happen to his mind. This effort on behalf of the coming generation in a country where devotion to children is exceptionally strong is by no means an unimportant factor in reconciling the people to many of the hardships of their existence and in rallying them to the support of the régime.

The Decree of June 20, 1935, provided for the institution of the "Fascist Saturday." All wage-earners, including government employees—with a few specified exceptions, such as the public utilities and other services that cannot conveniently be interrupted— must terminate their work on Saturday not later than 1 P.M. The total number of hours per week is not reduced, and the hours made free on Saturday are to be compensated for by extra hours on other days without extra pay; collective labor contracts are to be amended accordingly after consultation with the Secretary of the Fascist Party. The "Fascist Saturday" is to be devoted to military exercises, and to sports and activities of political, vocational and educational character. How extensive is the program of such activities appears from the fact that not only Saturdays but also Sundays are filled with them. The decree specifically provides that at least *one* Sunday per month must be free from all official or semi-official engagements.

M. Rosenstock-Franck, an outspoken critic of Fascism, expresses the opinion that in Italy the matter of salary has lost something of its importance since life in common has been occupying an ever-increasing amount of the worker's time. It is on the State and the Party that he largely depends today for his recreations, and the State and the Party see to it that they are handled in the proper spirit. "Nothing is more certain," writes M. Rosenstock-Franck, "than that these social organizations will ensure the harmonious physical development of the Italian race; and it is just as true that they will strengthen those moral virtues which grow out of team work (*vie d'équipe*)—audacity, self-sacrifice and gaiety. But they have killed all possibility of political education." If this analysis is correct Mussolini has arrived at one of his chief objectives.

INDUSTRIAL RELATIONS IN GERMANY

The labor policy of National Socialism developed, as was to be expected, along lines similar to those of Italian Fascism, with certain characteristic deviations due largely to the already familiar difference in the attitude of the two movements toward the class struggle. This difference, to repeat, consists in the acceptance by Fascism of the existence of a conflict of interests between capital and labor, a conflict which is completely denied by National Socialism.

"If in the future we are asked the question, What do you consider your greatest achievement?" Hitler declared in October 1933, "I can only answer: We have been successful in restoring the German worker to the Nation." The first step toward this object was the destruction of the German trade union movement which has in the past been the stronghold of the Social Democrats and, to a lesser degree, of the Communists. Preliminary measures with that object had been taken even in the days of the Weimar Republic, when the National Socialist Party had proceeded to establish a National Socialist Cell Organization (*Nationalsozialistische Betriebszellen Organisation*) which would fight the trade union movement from within. Early in May 1933 after the rise of Hitler to power, all the existing trade unions were taken over by the National Socialists and incorporated in one vast organization known as the Labor Front (*Deutsche Arbeitsfront*), under the leadership of Dr. Robert Ley; and his personal initiative, it would seem, had gone far toward giving the trade unions their *coup de grace*. Within the Labor Front, however, the trade unions, whose number has been greatly reduced through reorganization, continue to retain their identity. The former leaders of the trade unions were, of course, removed and not a few of them found themselves behind prison bars or in concentration camps. The Labor Front is much more than a mere professional association. It is officially described as the "organization of Germans engaged in productive work, whether of brain or hand" (*Organisation der schaffenden Deutschen der Stirn und Faust*). It comprises therefore not only workers and employees but also, as we know, all employers of labor, small artisans and members of liberal professions. Membership in the Labor Front, which is closed to non-Aryans, is a necessary qualification for any position in Germany today. The few loopholes that were left open in the

early months of the régime have been rapidly closed.
No wonder that in the beginning of 1935 the Labor
Front had, by official estimate, 23 million members,
while the 169 trade unions and their federation in
1932 had merely a rough 5 million members. The
organization of the Labor Front, which is one of
extreme complexity, is still very much in a condition
of flux, and is being constantly remodelled. I was
told so at its headquarters in Berlin in the summer
of 1935. It closely follows the structure of the
National Socialist Party. An official description issued at the end of 1934 states that the organization
of the Labor Front is based on the idea of the supremacy (*Primat*) of the Party. The first aim of the
Labor Front is the "ideological education of its
members in National Socialism." The field of its
economic activities is less well defined, and the matter has not been made simpler by the incorporation
in the Labor Front of the Reich Chamber of Economics. But one thing is certain: the National Socialist Party controls the labor organizations of Germany as completely as the Fascist Party controls
labor in Italy. The Labor Front, moreover, is based
on the principle of leadership, that is, the appointment of all officers by their respective superiors,
although the difference between this system and the
Fascist "elections," followed by official approval of
the candidates, is for all practical purposes nil.

The dependence of labor on the government has
been further increased by two legislative measures
enacted early in 1935. The Law of February 26, 1935,

provided for the introduction of "labor passports" (*Arbeitsbücher*) the purpose of which was stated to be "a more rational distribution of labor through Germany's economic system." The labor passport, the introduction of which has been left to the discretion of the Ministry of Labor, will contain a complete record of the worker's career. It was believed that this measure would first be applied to industries connected with the national defense and would thus make easier the mobilization of industry in case of some military emergency. The second law empowered the Minister of Labor to order employers to dismiss all workers who were formerly employed in agriculture; the desired effect was, first, that the latter would be forced to return to the farms thus lessening the shortage of skilled agricultural labor, and, second, that new jobs would be created in industrial centers where unemployment was particularly marked. These measures tend to curtail the freedom of the worker to choose the kind of labor that he likes best.

The Law of January 20, 1934, for the Organization of National Labor, which consolidated a number of legislative measures enacted during the preceding months, is probably the most characteristic document dealing with social policies that has so far come from the Hitler régime. It represents a practical attempt to carry into the troubled field of industrial relations that principle of national solidarity and classlessness which is the very essence of National Socialist ideology. The Law completely rejects the familiar conception that employers and employees are two elements in the process of production whose interests are frequently in conflict. "In every enterprise," says Article 1, "the owner, as the leader (*Führer*) and the salaried or wage-earning employees, as his followers (*Gefolgschaft*), shall work together for the furtherance of the purpose of the enterprise and for the benefit of the Nation and of the State." The leader is to make the decisions "in all matters that affect the establishment. He shall promote the welfare of his followers. The latter shall be loyal to him as fellow members in the common enterprise (*Betriebsgemeinschaft*)." This principle of cooperation finds its practical expression in the creation of a shop council (*Vertrauensrat*) consisting of not less than 2 and not more than 10 men representing the workers. The qualifications and method of election of these delegates (*Vertrauensmänner*) are highly characteristic. The candidate must be "a member of the Labor Front, possess exemplary qualities as a man, and must have given definite proofs of his unreserved devotion to the National Socialist State." The list of candidates is prepared by the owner and must be approved by the leader of the National Socialist Cell. It is then submitted to the vote of the workers, who may approve or reject it. In case of rejection the council is appointed by the Labor Trustee (*Treuhänder der Arbeit*). The duties of the council are to "strengthen mutual confidence within the enterprise and also to participate in the elaboration of measures designed to increase the efficiency of the concern. It must likewise take part in the preparation of shop rules and in the settling of disputes that may arise within the establishment, and also in promoting the welfare of the workers." The Law provides for a new official, the Labor Trustee, an office which was first established by the Law of May 19, 1933. The Labor Trustees, one for each industrial subdivision of the Reich, are appointed by the Government. Their chief task is "the maintenance of industrial peace." They also have jurisdiction in such matters as the dismissal of workers and the organization of shop councils. They supersede the owner of the enterprise in the decision of rates of wages, if the scale "appears to be incompatible with the economic and social conditions of the establishment."

A noteworthy innovation in the Law is the creation, in every labor trustee district, of a "court of honor" (*Ehrengericht*) consisting of a judiciary officer, appointed by the Minister of Justice, and two assessors—one an employer and one a member of the shop council—selected from a special list prepared by the Labor Front. These courts have jurisdiction over offenses that are considered a breach of "social honor." According to the Law every employer or worker "shall conduct himself in such a manner as to show himself worthy of the respect due to him as a member of the common enterprise. In particular he shall devote all his powers to the service of the establishment and the common good, always bearing in mind his responsibility." A breach of these obligations makes the offender liable to an appearance before the court of honor. A specific instance, mentioned in the Law, is in the case of the employer, "abuse of his authority by maliciously exploiting labor or wounding the sense of honor of the workers." In the case of the workers the Law refers particularly to "activities endangering industrial peace," "frivolous and unjustifiable complaints to the labor trustee," "intentional and unjustifiable interference of shop council delegates with the work of the enterprise and malicious disturbance of the community spirit," and, finally, "disclosure by shop council delegates of professional and trade secrets and confidential information." Penalties imposed by the courts of honor include warnings, reprimands, fines up to 10,000 marks, removal of the owner and dismissal of the employee. There is a right of appeal to a special court of appeal. The Law also contains a number of elaborate provisions designed to protect the worker from abrupt and unjustified dismissal.

The Law of January 20, 1934, behind its romantic, untranslatable and somewhat naïve phraseology glorifying the spirit of common endeavor, discloses the same preoccupation of the legislator observable in every important measure of Fascism and National Socialism—insistence upon the Party's absolute and supreme control of the entire machinery for the settlement of labor disputes. Employers and labor are unreservedly at the mercy of political appointees, such as labor trustees, members of the courts of honor, and delegates to the shop councils. The workers have lost the right of collective bargaining and the right to strike. The employer sees his hands tied by the constant supervision of representatives of the National Socialist Party and knows that he can be removed at any time for "malicious abuse of his authority." His freedom to establish wages has, in practice, remained a dead letter. Although the elaborate system of collective labor agreements that existed before 1933 was officially discarded, wages have, in general, been maintained on the old level by the decisions of the labor trustees. As in Fascist Italy, the radicalism of National Socialism is by no means dead and the employers are aware of the fact.

Information on the practical working of the machinery is scarce. Open labor disputes are definitely a thing of the past. The elections to the shop councils that took place in April 1934 were—though it became known only in 1935—not too encouraging for the régime. Only 40 per cent of the workers took part in the voting and many councils had to be appointed by the labor trustees. In the election of April 1935, however, about 80 per cent of the total number of workers and employees came to the polls and 83 per cent of them voted for the lists submitted by the employers. Under pressure, no doubt, but the machinery seems to work.

Information as to the working of the courts of honor is also meager. Between May 1, 1934, when the new law went into operation, and January 1, 1935, 61 cases have been referred to these courts. Of this number 56 were brought against employers, and only 5 against wage-earners. Of these 5, 3 were against executive officers (*Aufsichtspersonen*). Of the 56 cases against employers 22 were based on alleged offenses against the honor of the employees, 15 on "exploitation" of labor, and the balance on disregard of written orders of the labor trustees. Only 13 cases were decided before January 1, 1935. In 3 instances the employers were disqualified for further control of their businesses; and in 2 wage-earners (it is not clear whether they were executive officers or workers) were dismissed. The other cases resulted in fines and lesser penalties. The number of cases is too small and the courts have been in operation for too short a time to offer a basis for generalizations, but the nature of the few decisions so far rendered has probably contributed to the stimulation of the National Socialist zeal of the employers.

LABOR UNDER NATIONAL SOCIALISM

The striking growth of the Hitler movement since 1929 has in no small degree had its source in the economic and industrial condition of Germany in the years of the depression. National Socialism was actively supported by the unemployed, especially by the younger generation, whom the Führer had promised, with all the power of his savage eloquence, to show a way out of the bleakness of the present into a brighter future, where places will be assured for every man and woman willing and able to work. The struggle against unemployment and, even more—its complete wiping out—has been both the watchword and the set policy of the régime since it came into power. The leader of the Labor Front, Dr. Ley, declared in a speech in the spring of 1935 that before May 1, 1936, unemployment in Germany will have wholly disappeared. Hitler, addressing untold thousands of his countrymen at the Tempelhof demonstration of May 1, 1935, was more cautious. He merely promised that the Government would continue its struggle against unemployment until no longer should there be anyone without a job.

The Germans claim that the great effort made by the country to provide work for a very large number of its citizens has been crowned with complete and unqualified success. Official figures show a decline in the number of unemployed from over 6 million on January 30, 1933, to 1.7 million on September 1, 1935. According to a statement issued by the German Institute for Business Research (*Institut für Konjunkturforschung*) the struggle against unemployment up to September 1935 may be divided into four periods. (1) From the autumn of 1932 to the middle of 1933 the industrial situation began to show improvement, indicating that the low point of the depression had been passed. The first measures to create employment, taken by Hitler's predecessors, resulted in an increase in employment that averaged 67,000 a month. (2) The second period, covering about a year, from the middle of 1933 to the middle of 1934, gave an average monthly increase in employment of some 168,000 and made plain the full effect of the Hitler employment program. (3) The third period, from the middle of 1934 to November 1934, was characterized by a slowing down of the increase in the growth of employment, which at that time averaged 69,000 a month. (4) The fourth period, from November 1934 to September 1935, showed a new revival in the increase of employment, which was due to the launching of the Government's armament program. Its results have been felt with especial strength since the spring of 1935. As computed by the Institute for Business Research, the total of *regular* employment has increased from 11,470,000 in January 1933 to 16,350,-000 in July 1935. To this must be added 560,000 who were occupied in *substitute* employment ("land-helpers," the Labor Service, emergency and relief workers) which, for July 1935, gives a grand total of employment of 16,910,000. The corresponding figure for January 1933 was 11,730,000, thus giving a net increase in employment of some 5.2 million. The Institute for Business Research also points out that the number of emergency and relief workers (*Notstands- und Fürsorgearbeiter*) has declined from the high mark of 660,000 in March 1934 to the new low level of 200,000 in August 1935. According to the same authority the original projects, which have been mainly responsible for the rise in employment, are now being gradually completed, and their place is being taken by the new rearmament orders. The transition from employment projects to rearmament, we are told, occurred without any serious friction since both affect employment in much the same way. It may be added that they are also financed from the same source, that is, by the Government. The Institute, moreover, ventures the opinion that employment has already reached a high level, and that an increase of unemployment, rather than a further decrease, is to be expected in the coming months, as a partial consequence of the suspension of seasonal work in the course of the winter.

I am aware that German statistics of employment and unemployment have been subject to severe criticism and that their reliability has been questioned, not only by German *émigrés* but also by so authoritative a publication as the London *Economist*. It is impossible for me to go into the details of this controversy, in which the difficult question of "invisible" unemployment plays an important part. I have, nevertheless, taken considerable pains to ascertain the validity of the German figures, and have obtained the advice of some of the experts who used to be closely connected with the official German statistical agencies but were forced to leave the country on the establishment of the Hitler régime. I had also the benefit of the opinion of a foreign observer residing in Germany whose business it is to follow the economic development of the country. On the ground of information thus obtained I came to the conclusion that German employment and unemployment data are reasonably reliable, and that they at any rate give a fair picture of the general trend, even if the accuracy of some individual figures may be questioned. I see no reason, therefore, to doubt the large decrease in unemployment. Indeed, even if all statistics be put aside, increase in employment is suggested by the Government's present vast employment and rearmament program.

In dealing with unemployment the Government showed much determination and resourcefulness. The backbone of its employment program consisted of public works, including housing, highway construction, land reclamation and other projects. And, since the end of 1934 rearmament has loomed large in the picture. The Labor Service has for two years given employment to something like 500,000 men. The "Land-helpers" (*Landhilfe*), young workers chiefly from industrial areas, who receive a nominal wage and upkeep, are sent to assist the owners of medium-sized farms. In the fiscal year 1934–1935 their number was estimated at 160,000. Various measures have been introduced to encourage work-sharing. A limitation of the use of machinery in certain industries such as cigar and button making and Thuringia's glass industry, have been brought about by "voluntary" resolutions under official pressure. The same principle has made practicable the employment of the largest possible number of men by reducing to a minimum the use of machinery in public works. A revision of the income tax law permits the owners or directors of industrial plants to omit from their tax totals sums spent on the purchase of "short-lived" equipment, or, more exactly, equipment that probably would not last for more than five years. The purpose of this measure was to put a premium on immediate purchase of such equipment and thus increase employment. Employment of extra domestic servants was encouraged by making a special income tax allowance for any new servant so employed. The Government also enacted a number of measures providing for the substitution of male labor for female. There was no actual prohibition of the employment of women; but girls who gave up their positions and married received a loan of 1,000 marks from the Government, and the loan became a gift if she had children. This was a measure that also contributed to the revival of the furniture and household equipment industries. As for government employees and officers of public utilities, it was made obligatory on them to prevent their wives and children from taking employment.

In its desire to reduce unemployment the Government went so far as to sacrifice some of its most sacred principles. The campaign against department stores and even for a time, against some of the Jewish firms, was slowed down when it was realized that such a policy would necessarily lead to an increase in the number of the jobless. Dr. Goebbels resigned himself to tolerate a flagrant violation of one of National Socialism's ethical first principles, of which he is the custodian. Dr. Goebbels, as has been said, controls through the Reich Chamber of Culture and the Advertising Council, the entire business of publicity. His ethical code of advertising contains a provision prohibiting the use of superlatives that may be deemed detrimental to the sale of other similar products. A well-known firm had, as it happened, been for years describing one of its products as "the best." Its managers were ordered to destroy the containers that carried the offensive legend. The firm appealed to the Minister of Propaganda and explained that they had on hand and ready for delivery a very large stock of the product in question, and that the prohibition of its sale would force them out of business with, as a necessary consequence, increased unemployment. Accordingly, permission to carry on as before was graciously granted, and National Socialist ethics had, at least for a time, to bow before expediency.

The drafting into regular employment of a very large number of workers, especially of young people, thus removing them from the waiting lines at the employment offices, was undoubtedly an achievement of great social value and importance. But to a certain extent it was purchased at some cost to the working population at large. It has often been pointed out that the increase in the number of those employed was not accompanied by a proportionate increase in the nation's earned income. The work-sharing program and the fact that the very rapid absorption of the unemployed meant an increase particularly in the lower wage group are in part an explanation of this anomaly. But even if we accept such an explanation the fact remains that standard wages have been held at their former level while the index of the cost of living (1913–1914=100) has increased from 117.4 in January 1933 to 124.5 in August 1935, in spite of the Government's efforts to keep it stable. The quality of some of the articles of general consumption, especially those of the cheaper grades, has deteriorated considerably as a result of the shortage of raw materials and the necessity of using substitutes. This applies to textiles, chocolate, soap and many other articles. A shortage of certain foodstuffs, which developed in the autumn of 1935, has added to the difficulties of people with small incomes. In the meantime wages are maintained at a very modest level. In accordance with the report for 1934 of the I. G. Farbenindustrie, one of the leading concerns that employ a large percentage of skilled labor, the average weekly wage per worker was only 25 marks or, at the gold parity of the mark, about $10. From this modest income must be deducted payments on account for health and unemployment insurance, an income tax, and more or less "voluntary" contributions to the various social and charitable organizations of the National Socialist Party. It was generally expected that the Government would have to make some vital declaration regarding wages on the occasion of the celebrations of May 1, 1935. But this expectation was disappointed except in so far as Dr. Ley promised that a study of the problem of the "fair wage" would be undertaken in the course of the year, and that a definite proposal would probably be ready by May 1, 1936.

The leader of the Labor Front, however, looks upon wages in a way that is characteristic of National Socialism. "The main issue with the workman is not his ridiculous wage-pennies but the dignity of his position," Dr. Ley is reported to have declared to the Saar miners at Neukirchen in the early autumn of 1935, "and ultimately wage-questions settle themselves if the worker is left his self-respect. In the last resort the miner cannot be paid with money at all. What he receives is only a petty remuneration for his unremitting labor. It is therefore all the more ridiculous for people to begin to haggle about such little things." There is no way of knowing what the Saar miners thought about this speech, but that such a statement was made by the leader of the Labor Front is highly significant.

If National Socialism has thus far failed to improve the economic position of the masses of German labor it is largely due to the general economic difficulties experienced by the country. It is, however, realized by National Socialist leaders that to talk of the dignity of labor is not enough, even in a country like Germany where dignity and duty have an almost irresistible appeal. There is no reason to doubt the sincere interest of the Hitler Government in the welfare of labor, provided that it is promoted in accordance with the principles of the *Weltanschauung*. One of the chief agencies through which this interest has manifested itself is the organization affiliated with the Labor Front, the *Kraft durch Freude* ("Strength through Joy"). It is the German counterpart of the Italian *Dopolavoro* and it has accomplished some very good results in providing the working people with opportunities for sports, recreations, cultural activities and the like. In the course of 1934 the "Strength through Joy" organized holiday trips for some 2 million workers. The visiting of the beauty spots of Germany, to the accompaniment of much publicity and speech-making, is a part of the national education of every German today. As many as 80,000 people were taken on German vessels and at very low rates on trips to England, the Scandinavian countries and Spain. These activities would be even more admirable if they were not accompanied by a ceaseless "education" in the ideas of National Socialism and also, perhaps, if they were a trifle less noisy. I remember a rather miserable week-end at Nuremberg when I could get no sleep at all after about 5 A.M. The enthusiastic columns of the exuberant members of the "Strength through Joy," in military formation and at brief intervals, kept going by under the windows of my hotel, and at the top of their voices all were singing martial songs with changeless refrains that extolled *"Kraft durch Freude."* I finally got up in despair, feeling very weak and morose indeed.

There is also the highly popular and much advertised movement for the improvement of the physical surroundings of factories, workshops, and other places of employment. It is called "Beauty of Work" (*Schönheit der Arbeit*) and makes a strong appeal to the German worker, who has always been fond of both neatness and flowers. In these small improvements he sees evidence of the interest the Government and the Party are taking in his welfare; and perhaps he also sees a promise of greater things in the future. Germany's young people are certainly not forgotten, and they are brought up in the idea of boundless devotion to the Führer and the country under the banners of the Hitler Youth organization (*Hitler-Jugend*). About 6 million boys and girls of from 10 to 18 years of age were enrolled in 1934. They have their summer colonies and camps, their clubs and gymnasiums, their discipline, uniforms, badges, banners, bands and parades, a great deal of fresh air and healthy exercise, and, of course, a very large dose of National Socialist ideology.

All this might go a long way to make one believe in Dr. Ley's theory that wages, after all, are not the most important thing.

THE BALANCE-SHEET

Although between Fascism and National Socialism there are some notable differences in the approach to the question of industrial relations the fundamental factors in the policies they have adopted for the elimination of class warfare are really identical. Class struggle in the last analysis is a manifestation of the freedom of the individual to create for himself a place in the sun. It can be mitigated to a certain extent by the long and painful process of making people realize the interdependence and community of their varying interests; but it is doubtful whether it can be removed altogether without at the same time destroying the freedom of the individual. This is exactly what Fascism and National Socialism have done. Despite the grandiloquent declarations of the leaders and their eulogies of the "corporate spirit" and "national solidarity," in both Italy and Germany the entire machinery for the maintenance of peace between capital and labor rests wholly on the supremacy of Government and Party. And in both countries they have carefully weeded out every vestige of potential opposition. Labor disputes are the wretched and sinister products of capitalist society, and it is usually labor that suffers most. But the price at which industrial peace has been purchased in Italy and Germany seems altogether too high. And no amount of social work, however commendable in itself, not even the success of Germany in reducing unemployment, can disguise the fundamental fact that employers and labor in the two countries are today at the complete mercy of either the Fascist or the National Socialist Party.

CHAPTER VI

THE STATE AND THE FARMERS

THE IDEOLOGICAL FOUNDATION

"It is to the land that the hopes and energies of the peoples must turn, to draw from this primary source of all prosperity, from this ever renewed reservoir, the regenerating powers which will restore to the world its serenity and its wealth." In these words Mussolini expressed the fundamental beliefs that determine Fascist policy in regard to the farmer. Fascism sees in the rural community the chief mainstay of the State, and the assurance of the continuous and harmonious development of the Nation. The peasants are pictured as a robust and healthy population, the depository of that national, secular wisdom and moral force that originates in tradition and is handed down from generation to generation. By maintaining a high birth rate they provide the country with the bulk of its man power; they treasure the ancient virtues of thrift, love of the land, and devotion to church, home and family. It is the mighty stream of fresh blood coming from the countryside that rejuvenates our industrial civilization and saves it from complete decay. Agricultural work is a great deal more than merely a way of earning a living. It is also a social duty and, as a Fascist writer has put it, "a school of sacrifice and morality," for the peasant struggles unceasingly against the unpredictable manifestations of the uncontrollable forces of nature. Labor in the field is a mission. It received deserved honors in ancient times, when the land and its fertility were the objects of religious cults, and had their temples, their priests and their sacred rites.

Fascism believes, therefore, that it is the duty of the State to devote all its resources and all its energies to promoting the well-being of the tillers of the soil. At the same time Fascism holds that it is also the duty of the State to make certain that the country is in a position to provide enough of the essential foodstuffs to meet its domestic needs. This feeling is inspired not only by considerations of national safety in case of a military emergency, but also by the compulsion of national honor and self-respect. Thus the two principles on which Fascist agricultural policy is based become apparent: the recognition of the vital importance of the man on the land to the progress and development of the community, and the desire to make his harvests adequate to supply his country's demands.

National Socialism is, if possible, an even more enthusiastic worshiper of the mystic virtues of the rural community than is Fascism. It has already been said that many of the difficulties met with by post-war Germany are ascribed by National Socialist writers to the excessive industrialization of the country since 1870. This, they claim, resulted in the breakdown of the equilibrium between agriculture and industry; it led to the rapid growth of an urban proletariat crowded in the tenements of the great cities where they fell an easy prey to the hated "Marxists"; it increased Germany's dependence on foreign markets, jeopardized the military preparedness of the Nation and sapped its fighting power when war had been declared. More than that, the neglect of agriculture, needless to say, undermined the very source of the race, and diluted that vigorous blood the safeguarding of which is one of National Socialism's most sacred aims. "The possibility of preserving a sound peasantry as the foundation of the whole Nation," writes Hitler in *Mein Kampf,* "cannot be estimated too highly. Many of our present evils are the result of the unhealthy relationship between the rural and urban population. A solid bloc of peasants on their own small or medium-sized farms has been throughout the ages the best guarantee against social afflictions of the kind we are suffering from today. The existence of such a group is also the one thing that can make it possible for a Nation to earn its daily bread within the limits of its own economic organization." No wonder, therefore, that in Germany, during the first three years of the Hitler régime, government action went further in the aid of agriculture than it did in any other branch of economic life.

Glorification of the tiller of the soil, like any other principle of Fascism and National Socialism, cannot be accepted without marked reservations, if it can

be accepted at all. Is it true that close and daily
contact with the soil necessarily breeds those sturdy
and magnificent virtues which are so eloquently extolled by Mussolini, Walther Darré and so many
others? Like most city dwellers whose experience
of the country is limited to a few hurried week-ends
and a few quite as hurried summer weeks by the sea
or in the mountains, I often have an almost irresistible longing for the wide open spaces; especially on
some mellow spring or autumn evening when,
emerging from the eternal gloom of the subway, one
suddenly catches through the canyons of the towers
of Manhattan a glimpse of a magnificent sunset,
seemingly so out of place in its big city setting. I
feel, therefore, rather inclined to idealize country
life and like to imagine that a day will come when
I, too, will be able to settle down on a patch of land
and live happily among dogs, eggplants, cabbages
and potatoes. Literature is full of glowing descrip-
tions of rural life which fit beautifully into the picture traced by the Fascist and National Socialist
leaders. Turgenev's *Sportsman's Sketches* and
Hémon's unforgettable *Maria Chapdelaine* are
only two examples taken at random from hundreds.
But do they give a true picture or the whole picture?
For we have also *The Village* by Ivan Bunin, a
recent Nobel Prize winner, and we also have
Tobacco Road. Both in peace and in war I have
had opportunities to make close-quarter observa-
tions of peasant life in various parts of Russia, and
in Poland, Rumania, Galicia, France, England, Ger-

many and Italy. There are, no doubt, many country districts that would seem to bear out Fascist and National Socialist contentions. But there are also many others, especially in Eastern Europe, in certain parts of Germany, and in the mountain regions of France and Italy where one finds none of the admirable physical, moral and social qualities which are taken for granted by Walther Darré. Indeed it is impossible to imagine a life bleaker, more brutal and more lacking in all redeeming features than the one which in many places is lived by the peasantry. I understand that this is also true of the conditions that prevail in the cotton-growing sections of some of the Southern States. Contact with the soil has not, then, magical effects in every case, and the question inevitably arises whether the second part of the National Socialist formula, "Blood and Land" (*Blut und Boden*) is not as empty of real meaning as the first.

It may be just as well that no such doubts are permitted to interfere with the farm policies of Fascism and National Socialism, although measures for the relief of farming do not necessarily depend on any idealization of the rural community.

BONIFICA INTEGRALE

Mussolini's great effort for the rehabilitation of agriculture took the form of a comprehensive plan known as "integral land reclamation" (*bonifica integrale*). In order to realize the significance of the

measures taken it must be remembered that while
Italy has more than her share of beauty and sunshine, her soil is extremely unfitted for agriculture.
Mountain ranges occupy a considerable part of the
peninsula, and there are many large barren and
marshy areas which are unsuitable for cultivation
and are also poisonous with malaria. This was one
reason why some 9.5 million Italians have been
practically forced to emigrate and endeavor to make
a living in the United States, in South America and
in other parts of the world. To stop this stream of
emigration is one of the purposes of the Fascist
régime. The first measures for land reclamation go
back to 1882 and were concerned chiefly with the
draining of marshes and the carrying out of various
hydraulic projects. In the years following, this policy
of technical land improvement was accompanied by
measures for home colonization and the conversion
of the reclaimed land into small holdings. It was
not, however, until the advent to power of the Fascist Government that land reclamation became a
general and comprehensive policy. It has been carried into effect by a series of laws and decrees of
which the Decree of December 30, 1923, the Law of
May 18, 1924, the so-called "Mussolini Law" of December 24, 1928, and the Decree of February 13,
1933, are the most important.

The "integral" character of Fascist land reclamation is made evident by its program which provides
for the draining of marshes, the elimination of
malaria, such enrichment of the soil as will make it

suitable for agriculture and the colonization of the land so reclaimed. This last step in the program involves the building of farmhouses and roads and the arranging for water supplies. The plan is dealt with as an entity. It has for its purpose the establishment of new agricultural centers, the providing of means of existence for the largest possible number of farmers, and the bringing about of a more even distribution of the population, which, in its turn, will relieve the most congested areas. The projects comprised in integral land reclamation are divided into two groups: those recognized as primarily of value to the country at large and those primarily of benefit to local landowners. The character of the work undertaken may be similar in both cases; the difference in classification is based essentially on the varying degree of public usefulness involved, as also upon the fact that the projects of the first group must be carried out jointly, as a part of the general plan, while those of the second can be executed separately. It may likewise be true that the projects in the public interest involve a radical change in the existing methods of production while those of immediate benefit to local landowners merely provide for the betterment of farming methods already in use. But it may be questioned whether the latter distinction is always evident. In any case this division into two categories is of great practical importance. For the projects recognized as being primarily public are carried out at the expense of the State, with some assistance from local owners, while projects that are primarily of benefit only to the locality in question are carried out largely at its expense. The share of the State in financing land reclamation ranges from 75 to 92 per cent of the total cost of projects in the first group and is normally about 33 per cent in the case of the second. This latter percentage, however, is subject to important variations.

Participation in the execution of the projects decided upon is compulsory for all landowners in the area affected. And, since the local owners will be the first to benefit by the improvements, they are requested to contribute to the execution of the work. Indeed it is on the presumptive benefit to be derived by them from the work undertaken that the amount of their contributions is assessed. The execution of the work is usually entrusted to a local *consortium* or association which is made up of representatives of the local landowners and is at the same time an organ of the State. The State therefore reserves, and has widely used, the right to intervene in the affairs of the associations. Although the officers of the associations are supposed to be elected, their presidents must be confirmed by the Government. If, moreover, local landowners fail to organize an association for land reclamation such an agency is created by the Government irrespective of the wishes of the landowners.

The actual program for land rehabilitation in any particular district is usually determined by the local association for land reclamation; but not infrequently the initiative, and sometimes direct orders, come from the Government. All projects must be approved by the Minister of Agriculture and Forestry. The execution of the work is carried out either directly by the Government or, as is more usual, through the associations. They are made responsible for the financing of the projects in so far as they have been paid for by the contributions of the local landowners; and in the majority of cases the associations carry out that part of the work at the expense of the landowners. An owner who is unable or unwilling to meet charges assessed on him by the associations may either voluntarily transfer his property to someone willing to pay such charges, or his property is expropriated and he is indemnified according to its income value. This Fascist policy in the matter of land reclamation offers a good example of the attitude of the movement toward private property in general. The right of private property is maintained, but the owner is under obligation to use his land in a manner that the State considers desirable. If he fails to do so, his right in the property is destroyed, and it is transferred to someone who is willing to undertake what the Government considers to be the social obligations attached to ownership.

The State, however, denies all intention of undermining private ownership. Government intervention, it is argued, consists not in any attempt to remove private owners or to bring about the rigid regimentation of farming, but in directing the activities of the farmer into channels that are believed to be socially desirable. The State feels the more justified in doing so since it has invested large sums of public money in land improvements.

The program of integral land reclamation concerns itself not only with economic and social measures but also with questions of health and the distribution of population. In districts, for instance, that are afflicted with malaria a definite rotation of crops with the elimination of all pasture land may be enforced. Special types of farm buildings, designed to minimize the danger of malaria, may be made compulsory. It is a part of the policy to provide employment in agriculture for the largest number of people. Any methods of cultivation, therefore, which tend to reduce the volume of labor employed per hectare may be excluded. The average yield must also be maintained above a specified level. It is the aim of the Government to provide the farming people with stable and purely rural employment throughout the year. It is considered desirable, therefore, to establish newly created and independent farmers on plots of adequate size or, on large estates, to introduce a system of crop-sharing based on long-term contracts which will eliminate the employment of day-laborers. There is no hard and fast rule as to the exact relationship between the land and its tiller, but the intention of the legislation enacted is to make the connection permanent not only when the peasant has become an independent farmer or a tenant, but also when he works on a large estate. An agricultural laborer therefore

is visualized as a permanent employee living in a
cottage with his family, having a direct interest in
the produce of the land he is cultivating, and linked
to it not merely because it provides him with a living, but also by ties of natural affection. He is no
longer merely selling his labor by the hour or by the
day, but he is considered, as Signor Costanzo puts it,
"as a human being, a partner in the common enterprise." The policy of the Government in this respect
has been largely successful. In regions affected by
integral land reclamation the percentage of day-
laborers has vastly decreased, and in a number of
places it has disappeared altogether. The land rehabilitation program has also contributed to the reduction of unemployment, for the number of men employed on the various projects varied from an average of 33,000 in 1929–1930 to 71,000 in 1933–1934.

The centralizing tendency likewise makes itself
felt in the organization of the work of land rehabilitation. Since 1928 the local associations for land
reclamation have been compulsorily united into a
National Association. This is a Government controlled institution with broad powers in all matters
relating to land policy, especially in financing, which
is largely on a credit basis and is met by the issue of
special bonds guaranteed either by the State or by a
lien on the property of the individual landowner. A
transformation of the National Association into the
Fascist Institute for Land Reclamation was announced at the end of 1934, and was officially interpreted as a further step toward the strengthening of

the control of the Corporate State over the work of the local associations.

The Government has also been very active in improving land in mountain areas. This involved projects providing for afforestation, prevention of erosion, irrigation, and the like. The program of land improvement in all its ramifications represents what is for a poor country like Italy a very considerable financial effort. The entire expenditure for such purposes from 1922–1923 to July 1, 1934, has been officially estimated at 6,144 million lire, while only 1,782 million were spent on similar work from 1870 to 1922. The total area in which integral land reclamation had been carried through by July 1, 1934, was put at 4.7 million hectares,[1] and plans had then been prepared for the reclaiming of 3.4 million more. The bulk of the work has been done in the course of the last five years.

The most celebrated conquest by the *bonifica integrale,* and one much advertised, is the reclamation of the Pontine Marshes. The dismal appearance of this God-forsaken region is familiar to thousands of tourists, for it is crossed by the Appian Way, and few visitors to Italy miss it. The transformation that the Fascist régime has worked in converting the swamps and barren wastes of the *Agro Pontino* into honest farm land is truly miraculous, especially if one remembers that the work of reclamation was embarked upon only at the end of 1931. When, in August 1935, I visited the new agricultural settle-

[1] One hectare = 2.47 acres.

ments in this region, more than 41,000 hectares had been redeemed, and the remaining 2,000 hactares of marshes were about to disappear. The town of Littoria was founded in June 1932 and that of Sabaudia in August 1933. By the summer of 1935 they had become urban settlements with churches, hospitals, schools, government offices, all modernistic and a bit pretentious. While these two new towns naturally lacked the charm of the old Italian cities, they were, frankly, a great credit to the régime. Sabaudia, moreover, is pleasantly situated on the shores of Lake Paola, within easy reach of the Mediterranean. With its flat-roofed white houses and growth of palm trees it presented, under the burning sunshine of August, a distinctly tropical appearance. In 1935 about 60,000 people were living where once were the marshes. Land is divided into small holdings of from 10 to 30 hectares. The task of providing settlers is entrusted to the *Opera Nazionale Combattenti* (National Association of War Veterans) which, in spite of its name, is a purely Government agency. Most of the settlers come from the Province of Veneto which is particularly congested and the population of which is believed to be better fitted to withstand the danger of malaria. The new settlers usually have no capital and are provided by the *Opera Nazionale*, with a house, implements, stock, seed and so on. The only thing they bring with them is the old family furniture. Under their agreement with the *Opera Nazionale*, an agreement that covers the next 25 or 30 years, they turn over to it their entire harvest save what is needed for themselves and their farms. The *Opera Nazionale* keeps an account with each settler and credits him with payments for the amortization of his debt by converting into lire, and at current market prices, the agricultural produce he has grown and delivered. An average family consists of twelve or fourteen. One family, the Director of the *Opera Nazionale* told me, came with 24 sons. It was given the maximum allotment of 30 hectares, and certainly deserved it. The settlers live in separate four-room farmhouses which have stables attached. I was struck by the absence of such farm buildings as barns and was told that this was due to a shortage of funds. The several farms I visited would not impress anyone used to American standards, but they were undoubtedly a great improvement upon those the settlers had left behind them. No provision has thus far been made to prevent the breaking up of the holdings in the future. "We had no time to think about it," the Director remarked. Land varies in quality, and some of it is not very good; but much is being done to enrich it. The use of tractors is permitted for only the first year or two. After that—in order to provide employment for the largest possible number—cultivation is to be carried on by human labor with, of course, the help of the farm stock. The settlers certainly did not look prosperous, but they looked healthy, gay, as Italians so often are, and seemed to be willing to work hard. They know that if they do not live up to what is expected of them they will have to return to their former homes. A few such expulsions had actually taken place.

All things considered, the visit to the *Agro Pontino* left an extremely favorable impression. It cannot reasonably be doubted that in this field the Fascist régime is doing truly excellent work. The burden it imposes upon the Treasury, which, to repeat, is a heavy one for a poor country such as Italy, must also be borne in mind.

THE "BATTLE OF THE WHEAT"

The struggle to attain self-sufficiency in food-stuffs, especially in wheat, is the second pillar of the agricultural policy of the Fascist régime. The "Battle of the Wheat" was dramatically heralded by Mussolini at the night session of the Chamber of Deputies on June 25, 1925, a session to which Fascist writers like to refer as "historic." The Duce, of course, immediately assumed command and, with himself as chairman, he created a committee which he likes to call his General Staff. In 1910–1914 Italy had under wheat an average area of 4.7 million hectares which produced 48.7 million quintals,[2] or 10.4 quintals per hectare. Some 14.9 million quintals had to be imported. To grow this wheat at home became one of the aims of the régime. By the end of the three years, 1923–1925, immediately preceding the proclamation of the "Battle of the Wheat," the yield per hectare had already increased to 12.4 quin-

[2] One quintal = 220 pounds = 3.7 bushels.

tals, but imports still averaged 23.8 million quintals. As a result of the energetic measures taken by the Government the improvement now became a rapid one; and by 1933 the Government could proclaim the "Victory of Wheat," for in that year something more than 5 million hectares had produced an average of 15.9 quintals per hectare, a record crop, or 81 million quintals in all. Italy needed no more foreign grain and the occasion was celebrated with much solemnity. In 1934, however, unfavorable weather conditions resulted in a poor harvest, and although the area under cultivation—4.9 million hectares— was only slightly below that of the previous year, the total yield dropped to 63.4 million and the yield per hectare to 12.8; that is, very nearly as low as the level of 1923–1925. It would seem however that this was merely an accidental setback. The provisional estimate for the harvest of 1935, which appeared in *Il Messagero* on August 8, 1935, puts the total crop at 76.4 million quintals, and the average yield per hectare at 15.2. It is believed that the domestic supply of grain will be sufficient in 1935 to meet the requirements of the country.

Assuming that the average crop yields for 1931– 1933 will be maintained in the future, it would seem that the "Battle" has actually been won. But like all victories, it was purchased at a price. Some of the measures used to increase the yield and to expand the area under wheat have been perfectly justifiable and even commendable. Such, for instance, was the campaign to educate the farmer in the use of better seeds, implements and fertilizers. Here intensive propaganda was conducted by special organizations and by the associations of agricultural employers and workers under the leadership of their respective national confederations. Much publicity is now given to the annual "wheat contests" which are held in every province and also on a national scale, the latter in the presence of the Duce. A vast amount of propaganda literature, as well as exhibitions, experimental stations, travelling lecture-ships, training schools and the like serve the same purpose. Credit institutions come generously to the assistance of farmers who have embarked on a policy of improvements or who desire to purchase agricultural machinery. Foreign oil intended for the use of tractors and other machines was exempted from both import duties and the sales tax.

More effective, probably, but also much less unobjectionable, were the measures adopted by the Government to maintain the level of agricultural prices. Not only was an exceptionally high tariff imposed on imported wheat (since 1931 it has been 75 lire per quintal), but it was also provided that foreign wheat should not constitute more than a certain percentage of the total wheat milled. In June 1933 the proportion of domestic wheat was put at 99 per cent. It varied from time to time, but always remained very high. Similar restrictions were imposed on imported flour. Much has also been done to encourage the peasants to sell their wheat through specially built collective warehouses, where in 1934 they re-

ceived on delivery an advance of 75 lire per quintal
and 90 lire in 1935. The farmers were thus encouraged to withhold their stocks from the market in
order to raise prices. The millers were at the same
time put under obligation to purchase a given percentage of their supplies from the collective stores.
And the Government assumed responsibility for
part of the interest due on the sums advanced to the
farmer as wheat loans. The effect of these measures
was that while Italian wheat prices declined during
the depression, they continued to be considerably
above world prices. This was undoubtedly a hardship to the consumers in days of rapidly dwindling
incomes, especially in Italy where, with the low level
of wages, expenditure on staple foods means a very
large item in the worker's budget.

Measures taken by the Fascist Government for
the encouragement of crops other than wheat failed
to effect any striking changes. Steps were taken to
relieve the burden of farm indebtedness which, with
the continuance of the depression, had become un-
bearable. It may be said that in general the desire
of the régime to help the rural community was certainly in evidence, and full credit must be given to
Mussolini for his land reclamation program. But
the fact remains that the fate of the Italian tiller of
the soil is far from being a fortunate one. The earnings of agricultural labor, as we have seen, are appallingly low. On October 25, 1934, the national confederations of employers and workers reached an

agreement designed to eliminate the employment of day-laborers, who were to be put on a profit-sharing basis. Whether this change will lead to an improvement in the laborer's position is still uncertain. In the meantime the poverty of Italian peasants cannot but strike any observer who tries, when in Italy, to get away from the beaten roads. In the summer of 1935 I took several walking trips in the Central Apennines. The peasants, in their picturesque villages high up in the mountain and accessible only by narrow paths, live on the meager proceeds of tiny fields located not infrequently several hundred feet below the village itself. Their farms consist largely of rocks and little grows on them. The *contadino* and his mule appear to be inseparable, and both alike seem to be resigned to their endless and largely futile labor. Six or seven lire a day is all a peasant can hope to earn if and when he can get work. They eat meat once or twice a year. "*I contadini sono tutti poveretti*" ("Peasants are all poor") one of them told me with resignation, and the truth of the statement was only too obvious. It would be unreasonable to blame Mussolini for this state of affairs, which he inherited from the past. But it is this situation, I believe, that is at the bottom of Italy's East African venture. Italy's tariff policy, of course, is in a different class, although here, too, Mussolini merely followed in the footsteps of his predecessors. And since the League of Nations has applied economic sanctions to Italy the fostering of domestic

production of foodstuffs is regarded by many Ital
ians as the most striking manifestation of Mussolini's foresight and political genius.

HEREDITARY FARMS IN GERMANY

Although National Socialism has been at the helm
for a much shorter time than has Fascism the measures taken by the Hitler Government in the sphere
of agriculture have been a great deal more drastic
and far-reaching than those of Mussolini. This is
probably due in part to the fact that the Germans
take their slogan "Blood and Land" much more
seriously than the Italians take theirs. It is due also
in part to their more intense desire to escape from
dependence on foreign countries for their food supplies, a desire that finds a strong economic stimulus
in the foreign trade and exchange difficulties which,
since 1933, have become more and more pronounced.

The most spectacular innovation of the National
Socialist agrarian legislation is the Law on Hereditary Farms (*Reichserbhofgesetz*) of September 29,
1933.[3] It established the peasant farm (*Hof*) as a
hereditary farm (*Erbhof*) which cannot be sold,
mortgaged or disposed of by inheritance except in
the manner provided by the Law. In order to qualify
as a hereditary farm, a farm must meet certain conditions. It must be a self-contained economic entity

[3] The provisions of the Law were amplified and expounded in
the circulars (*Durchführungsverordnungen*) of October 10, 1933,
December 19, 1933, April 27, 1934, and January 4, 1935.

worked largely by the labor of the farmer's family.
In practice, however, all farms from 7.5 hectares to
125 hectares are classified as hereditary and larger
farms may be included under certain conditions. The
hereditary farm comprises not only land and farm
buildings, but also agricultural machinery, implements, livestock and the various supplies and reserve
capital necessary for the successful carrying on of
the agricultural enterprise. The owner of the hereditary farm has the title of *Bauer* (Peasant) which no
one else is permitted to use, all other landowners
being described by the term *Landwirt*. To be a peasant is now declared to be a most honorable position.
It can be conferred only on persons who can trace
their German ancestry back to 1800, a task which is
easier than would be expected because of the complete and excellent church records. A peasant must
also possess the qualities requisite to the proper
working of his farm (*Bauernfähigkeit*). The loss of
these precious qualities may result, under certain
conditions, in his removal from his hereditary farm
by an order of the hereditary court (*Anerbenge-
richt*). The right of succession to a hereditary farm
is carefully established by the law and is based on
the idea of retaining the property in the male line.
The order of succession is as follows: the sons of the
peasant; his father; his brothers; his daughters; his
sisters; any other descendants in the male line in
order of priority. The sons of the prospective heirs
take, in the order of succession, the place of their de-

ceased parent. The hereditary farm cannot be divided (a rule with just one exception) and it passes to a single heir. Which of the sons is to get the farm is decided by local customs, which favor either the eldest or the youngest. In the absence of any definitely established custom the youngest son receives the farm on the ground that this reduces the probability of a frequent change in ownership. In certain cases, which have their source in customary law, or on showing good cause, the peasant may enjoy a certain degree of testamentary freedom, but only with the approval of the hereditary court. The widow and the other dependents of the deceased peasant have a right to maintenance from the farm; minors are entitled to proper education and training; and all alike have the right to return to the farm in case of illness, disability or old age (*Heimatzuflucht*). For the loss of their share in the farm they are also entitled to compensation from the residue of the estate of the deceased, if there be such residue. The Law on Hereditary Farms introduces into peasant husbandry the principle of the Prussian *Fideikommisse* which, until 1919, regulated the succession of estates held by the nobility. The new legislation has three main purposes: to strengthen the link between the peasant and his farm; to eliminate the possibility of the breaking up of peasant holdings into small strips; and to relieve the peasant from the burden of mortgages and the danger of foreclosures.

So far as the first two of these objects were concerned the National Socialist Government had no special grounds for anxiety. The tradition of preserving the farm intact at the death of the head of the family is firmly rooted in German peasantry and has withstood the test of centuries. Their attachment to the native soil has been fully proved and hardly needs any special encouragement. According to Professor Sering, in the post-war period four-fifths of the German peasant farms were self-contained, compact holdings, jealously guarded against partition. The very small peasant holdings are to be found only in southwestern Germany, especially along the Rhine and in the country spreading northward into Thüringia. This difference in the forms of tenure goes back to the early Middle Ages. The smallness of the holdings in the south is due not to the evil effect of Roman Law and of the Code Napoleon introduced early in the nineteenth century, as is so often contended by National Socialist writers, but to the simple economic fact that the Rhineland is a vine-growing country where the intensive cultivation of small holdings is perfectly sound economically. It must also be said that the new National Socialist legislation, which claims to revert to the traditional forms of inheritance as practised in Germany from time immemorial, really infringes upon one of the fundamental rules of German customary law: the equal right of all children in their father's estate. Although this right is not specifically denied, under the prevailing conditions of farming the chance that the children who do not get the farm will obtain any substantial part of the estate is very small indeed. The new law also changes fundamentally the position of the widow, who is not even mentioned among the heirs, although she is legally entitled to maintenance.

As to relief from the burden of mortgages and the fear of foreclosure it must be pointed out that the financial difficulties that have been experienced of late by German farmers have been due only in a minor degree to indebtedness resulting from death settlements. According to Professor Sering, little more than one-quarter of the debt, amounting to some 13,000 or 14,000 million marks, incurred by German farmers since the end of inflation to 1932 originated in death settlements. This, of course, is not a negligible amount. But the complete withdrawal from the market of hereditary farms raises a number of complex questions. In accordance with the computations of the German Institute for Business Research the law affects about one million farms or 54 per cent of the total number. They cannot be sold or mortgaged, although the owners are made liable for the mortgages incurred in the past, which are being converted, at a considerable discount, into annuities. The question of agricultural credit immediately arises. Mortgage credit is obviously ruled out. It is to be replaced by a form of personal credit based on the productivity of the farm and also on the possibility that the farmer who fails to meet his obligations may forfeit his right to enjoyment on the ground that he has not shown the required diligence in administering the property. The question of new farm credit is still much discussed and awaits solution.

It may be said in general that the Law on Hereditary Farms did not bring any substantial changes in the order of peasant succession that prevailed over the largest part of Germany, with the exception of the southwest. The indivisibility of the farm was a rule that was generally enforced and that had behind it all the authority of tradition and customary law. It is too early to speak of the practical effect of the new legislation. Unquestionably, it came as a severe blow to the members of the well-to-do peasant families who suddenly found themselves faced with the unpleasant fact that they would get nothing from their fathers' estates. It seems likely that it will lead to efforts by the heads of families to invest less in their farms and build up capital funds from which their less fortunate heirs may be indemnified.

THE REICHSNAHRSTAND

Of much greater immediate consequence than the Law on Hereditary Farms was the complete reorganization of agriculture which followed the publication on September 13, 1933, of the Law on the "Agricultural Estate" (*Reichsnährstandgesetz*). It will be remembered that after the formation of the Hitler Government there was much talk about the building up of a German Corporate State, but that so far the plan had failed to materialize, with, however, one important exception. This exception was the "Agricultural Estate," a creation—like the Law on Hereditary Farms—of Walther Darré, who in the summer of 1933 succeeded Dr. Hugenberg as Minister of Food and Agriculture. "Agricultural Estate" is really a very inadequate translation of the German *Reichsnährstand*. Like the Italian corporations, the *Reichsnährstand* is a complex structure of associations, bureaus and boards based on the idea of a "cycle of production," in this case the production of foodstuffs. The Agricultural Estate, therefore, comprises all activities dealing with the production, processing and distribution of foodstuffs. It might have been better, perhaps, to call it "Food Estate" if the phrase did not sound so awkward in English. The Law of September 13, 1933, was merely the corner stone of the new organization which since that time has been expanded in innumerable laws, decrees and circulars.

The *Reichsnährstand* is a good example of the new type of organization that has come into existence in the Third Reich and that one finds very difficult to classify. It is, strictly speaking, neither a private corporation or association, nor an organ of the State, but combines the features of both. The *Reichsnährstand* has absorbed all the numerous associations and organizations connected with the production and distribution of foodstuffs that existed in Germany in the past. Membership in the *Reichsnährstand* is also compulsory for every individual who is engaged in any pursuit or trade concerned with foodstuffs. The *Reichsnährstand* is headed by the Reich Peasant Leader (*Reichsbauernführer*) appointed by the Chancellor. To add to the confusion, the present Reich Peasant Leader is Walther Darré, who is also Minister of Food and Agriculture. The *Reichsnährstand* is organized on the leadership principle; that is, Darré appoints the chief officers of the organization who, again, appoint their subordinates, and this is continued all down the line. The former autonomy of the agricultural associations, which would naturally be out of place in the totalitarian State, is completely gone. The fundamental principle of the new structure would seem to be that of voluntary cooperation between the Government and the trades and producers concerned. The Government, through the Minister of Agriculture, lays down the general lines of the policy which it is the duty of the *Reichsnährstand* to put into practice. To what extent the cooperation between the *Reichsnährstand* and the Government is voluntary is doubtful, and one may well wonder whether Darré himself can be certain when he is Minister of Agriculture and when he is Reich Peasant Leader. On the other hand, it is probably true that the local organs of the *Reichsnährstand* are largely representative of the interests of the producers and traders; but these interests, of course, are never permitted to interfere with what is believed to be the broader interests of the Nation. And this is a question which the Government, the National Socialist

Party and Darré himself have to decide. It was announced on October 6, 1935, that the *Reichsnähr-stand*, following the example of the Reich Chamber of Economics, had, as a body joined the Labor Front. It is uncertain at the time of writing whether this will not involve some limitation of the freedom of action the leader of the *Reichsnährstand* has enjoyed in the past.

The *Reichsnährstand* is an organization that is most extraordinarily involved. It consists of two separate sets of organizations. In one the divisions are territorial or horizontal; in the other they are vertical or according to trade. The whole territory of the Reich, for the purposes of the *Reichsnähr-stand*, is divided into 19 *Landesbauernschaften*, which are again subdivided into 514 *Kreisbauern-schaften* and many thousands of *Ortsbauernschaften*. The vertical organization consists of associations and boards which concern themselves with separate branches of husbandry such as grain, dairy farming, livestock, poultry, milk, cooperative societies, and so on. There is, of course, a great deal of overlapping and a certain amount of confusion. It is freely ad-mitted in Berlin even by the admirers of Darré that the organization has been built up too rapidly and needs a good deal of readjustment.

I had an interview with the Peasant Leader (*Bauernführer*) of *Landesbauernschaft Kurmark*, Bredow. He proved to be a real peasant, and very different from the university graduates on his staff. Herr Bredow received me in a brown suit, breeches and suspenders, and in his black tie he wore a large pin which carried the National Socialist emblem. He delivered, for my benefit, a political speech on the regeneration of Germany and the greatness of Hitler. I left him with the distinct impression that he was merely a figurehead, an impression that was confirmed by information from various sources.

In spite of its obvious imperfections the *Reichsnährstand* has proved to be an effective instrument for the control of German agriculture. The ultimate aim of this control is to create in Germany a balanced economy where the supply and demand of foodstuffs will be in a state of equilibrium. The practical measures have originated in the necessities of the moment, namely the need of maintaining the stability of agricultural prices, and also of developing those branches of agricultural production which might provide substitutes for commodities formerly imported from abroad. The already prohibitive tariff on imported foodstuffs has been further increased and new duties have been imposed on fats, eggs and bacon. Imports of butter had, in 1932, already been made subject to a quota. A series of decrees in 1933 and 1934 introduced a system of close supervision over the production and distribution of grains, fats, milk and dairy produce, livestock and meats, fruit and vegetables, potatoes and sugar. This system of supervision went much farther than anything that had been attempted in industry. Prices of the various foodstuffs were fixed by the Government. The millers received definite orders as to how much and what kind of grain they would be permitted to mill. The grades and prices of flour were also subjected to minute regulations. Every mill was, moreover, put under obligation to keep on hand a stock of grain representing not less than 150 per cent of its average monthly requirements for the preceding year. Farmers were to deliver at specified dates specified amounts of grain. By an ordinance of July 14, 1934, special associations for the production and sale of grain were established in each of the 19 regions into which the country is subdivided for the purposes of the *Reichsnährstand*. These associations were given the power not only to determine the exact amount of grain to be delivered by each producer and the place where it was to be turned over, but also to close for a time or altogether any wholesale or retail stores, mills, or bakeries which they considered economically unsound or undesirable. The owner of enterprises thus closed were entitled to an indemnity which was eventually to be provided by their competitors who had benefited by the measure. The same ordinance of July 14, 1934, introduced fixed prices for grain. The prices decreed in 1933 had been merely minimum prices; and the new prices were from 5 to 7 per cent higher than these minimum prices of 1933. This regulation involved a loss to the farmers; but this was, officially, held to be a voluntary concession on their part to the consumers and a manifestation of the spirit of "national solidarity." In the case of fats, eggs, butter, cheese and milk the Government created sales monopolies; that is, no such commodity was permitted to reach the market without the preliminary approval of an appropriate Government office. These sales-monopoly boards do no trading themselves, but they have ample means at their disposal for the regulation of the volume of supplies and the influencing of prices.

This brief survey of the State's intervention in the production and distribution of foodstuffs will suffice to give an idea of the far-reaching methods of the *Reichsnährstand*. There is some difference of opinion among the officials of the organization itself as to whether these measures should be held to be a definite policy or merely emergency legislation, due in part to the protracted drought which in 1934 caused great alarm in Germany. This, however, is not the opinion of Darré who declared early in 1934 that the system of control of agricultural production and prices might be used as a model for the application of similar methods of industry. It was hoped that some of the most vexatious measures of control might be abandoned in 1935, but these hopes have not been fulfilled.

As to the general effect of State control of agriculture it has largely succeeded in maintaining the level of prices, although this was probably achieved at a cost to the consumers. On the whole the system has worked fairly well, except for the so-called Fat Plan, which originated with Dr. Hugenberg and was designed to make Germany self-supporting in fats. The execution of this plan proved so costly that at the end of 1934 it had practically to be abandoned. Agricultural conditions in Germany are exceptionally favorable for State control. Supply and demand have been very nearly balanced, but not quite; and there is in foodstuffs a slight deficiency which is made good by imports. This offers practically ideal conditions for Government intervention. It is far less certain that it would be equally successful if tried in the field of industry.

THE RHÖN PLAN

The rapidly growing burden of agricultural indebtedness had been a matter of concern to the Government. Several measures for its reduction had been taken by Hitler's predecessors, beginning with 1931. A radical move in this direction was made by National Socialism in July 1933, when the whole structure of farm indebtedness and interest charges was drastically revised with a view to bringing them into line with the earning capacity of the farms. The Government here assumed heavy liabilities in order to relieve the situation of the mortgage banks, whose position would otherwise have been seriously affected. The farmers, moreover, benefited by a number of important readjustments in the system of taxation that were designed to encourage them to proceed with various improvements.

The National Socialist Government has also continued to maintain the policy of the Empire and the Weimar Republic in the matter of home colonization (*Bauernsiedlung*). There has been no attempt so far to expropriate the large estates and to convert them into small holdings. It has been the policy of the new Government to increase the average size of the holdings so as to bring them into the class of hereditary farms. This policy was merely the accentuation of a tendency that had already manifested itself in previous years. In 1934, 144,600 hectares were converted into small holdings, or more than in any previous year since the war. The new homesteads numbered 4,800. Of these 70.2 per cent were holdings of 10 and more hectares, and only 4.7 per cent of less than 2 hectares.

A characteristic venture of the National Socialist Government is the so-called Rhön or Dr. Hellmuth's plan. The Rhön is a small mountain region of volcanic origin bordering on Thüringia, Franconia and Hesse. Dr. Hellmuth is the National Socialist leader (*Gauleiter*) and President of the Government of Main-Franconia of which the ancient city of Würzburg, the former seat of the Prince-Bishop, is the capital. The Rhön is within Dr. Hellmuth's jurisdiction. For a number of historical reasons the Rhön is a very poor country. It has a population of some 130,000, and they lead a miserable existence chiefly by agriculture carried on by backward methods on narrow scattered strips of land. The people are crowded into small villages and hamlets at the foot of a chain of mountains or high hills. Rising to some 2,500 feet this mountain area had few roads and was neither inhabited nor cultivated. When the unhappy state of the Rhön in general came to Dr. Hellmuth's attention he conceived the idea that it offered an opportunity to put into effect some of the best ideas of National Socialism. This is how the Rhön or Dr. Hellmuth's plan came into being, and this is also the reason why I boarded a train in Berlin and betook myself to the ancient city of the Prince-Bishop.

The plan, as one would expect, is based on the idea of "Blood and Land." The Rhön mountain area is to be converted into fertile fields of the hereditary farm type which will be handed over to the local peasants and thus restore them to decent living and respectability. In order to achieve this truly commendable purpose roads are being built, marshes drained, and an extensive plan of afforestation—to offer protection against the winds—has been embarked upon. The work is carried on partly by the Labor Service and partly by local people who receive regular wages. One of the tasks of the Labor Service is to clear the fields or rocks and stones and thus prepare them for ploughing, a rather formidable and thankless job. In the colonization of the reclaimed land no compulsion of any kind, I was assured, is to be used. The new settlers will come forward voluntarily and will exchange their present scattered strips of land for the nice, compact holdings. Their former fellow villagers, who remain down in the valley, will also indirectly benefit by the new venture. There is nothing one could object to in this part of the plan, although one may be permitted to have certain doubts as to the extent to which the land recovered will prove suitable for grain growing or even make good pasture land. What I have seen of it would justify a guarded optimism.

But the National Socialist formula is a formula with two elements, "Blood and Land." And, meanwhile, the first of them has not been forgotten. There is in Würzburg a special bureau for matters of population and race policy. And I was there offered an opportunity to inspect some 16,000 files. They contained the family trees of that number of Rhön peasants. The family trees are prepared in the schools, by the children working under the supervision of the teachers. They are checked from the church and other records by a special staff and the information is also verified by interviews with the older members of the community. The purpose of this strange procedure, I was told, was not so much to detect non-Aryan strains—for there do not seem to be any Jews in the Rhön—as to examine the progenitors in question, from the point of view of health, inheritable or other diseases, general behavior, good morals, and so on. The information is further cross-checked by giving children intelligence tests the results of which, it was admitted, were sometimes disappointing. That is, children who had an excellent ancestry occasionally proved inferior, while those who were cursed with a drunken father and a depraved grandmother did unusually well. But the youthful investigator into race mysteries, who made these compromising admissions, expressed the hope that things might straighten out in the next generation. It is on the ground of this information that the eligibility of the Rhön peasant for the new farms will be decided. I remarked to the very kind and earnest head of the Würzburg office that it was not always possible to be certain of the paternity of a child. It took some time to make him admit the fact, but he then added hurriedly that such things did not happen in the Rhön. A couple of young S. A. and S. S. men who had been following our conversation seemed to be less sure about that than was the distinguished professor. Germany is, indeed, suffering from a strange obsession.

AGRICULTURE AND THE STATE

The balance-sheet of Italian and German agricultural policy is somewhat uncertain. There is no doubt that the two countries have made a very great effort to deal with the question of farming and food supply. They have been largely successful in achieving self-sufficiency in foodstuffs, although this success has been purchased rather dearly. Self-sufficiency in foodstuffs, moreover, is in no way peculiar to Fascism and National Socialism. The Weimar Republic had a similar objective and took a number of measures in this direction, especially in its later years.

The changes that have been brought about in the condition of farmers and agricultural laborers are less certain. They have been helped as producers by the respective government policies for the maintenance of the level of prices; but they have suffered as consumers from the resulting higher cost of living. They have also had to undergo an unusually large measure of government control and supervision. It may be no exaggeration to say that the right of land ownership has, in Italy and in Germany, suffered an important modification. Ownership of land is no longer regarded as an absolute right of property, but rather as a kind of trusteeship. It is an ownership that can be drastically interfered with, and even brought to an abrupt end, if the State considers that the owner does not perform what is believed to be his social duty. So far, actual instances of the more drastic forms of State intervention have been rare, but the change in attitude is unmistakable. And this attitude, from what we know of Fascism and National Socialism, is by no means incompatible with their ideology.

CHAPTER VII

THE NEMESIS: PUBLIC FINANCE AND FOREIGN TRADE

AUTARCHY

A DISCUSSION of the financial and commercial policies of Italy and Germany does not, strictly speaking, come within the scope of this volume for the simple reason that there is no such thing as the financial and commercial policy of a totalitarian State. No government, either democratic or dictatorial, not even that of the Soviet Union, has yet succeeded in harnessing the great economic forces that rule our complex civilization. A brief survey of the financial and economic situation in the two countries is nevertheless essential in order to complete the picture. For whatever one may choose to say about the primarcy of politics over economics, it is to the economic exigencies that, sooner or later, one has to bow. In striking contrast with the political, social and cultural programs of Fascism and National Socialism, their economic policies show a remarkable continuation of those of their predecessors. The changes that have taken place have largely been dictated by expediency and not by ideological considerations. It is not surprising, therefore, to find a striking similarity between the financial and economic measures of Fascism and National Socialism and those adopted in practically every other country, especially since the beginning of the depression. Prohibitive tariff barriers, the obstinate fostering of domestic industries at a heavy cost to the consumer, import and export licenses and quotas, government subsidies to industry, agriculture and shipping, public works, unbalanced budgets, surreptitious credit expansion, pressure on banks to make them absorb government securities, manipulation of currencies—all these familiar devices for capturing prosperity or doctoring economic evils are, unfortunately, by no means peculiar to dictatorial régimes. They can, indeed, under the most benevolent of democracies develop and flourish on a scale that no dictator has yet succeeded in even approaching.

One important point must be cleared up before we proceed any further. In both Italy and Germany much has been written in favor of autarchy or complete economic independence of the outside world. This objective has been advocated by the supporters of Fascism and National Socialism in part as an important step toward the creation of that ideal community in which all economic activities will be harmoniously balanced, and in part as a condition of national security in time of war. Germany has not forgotten the bitter lesson of the Allied blockade, which proved probably the most effective method of breaking down the resistance of the Central Powers.

And, since the application of economic sanctions by the League of Nations in November 1935, Italy has been learning the same bitter lesson. We know already that, from the beginning, the drive for self-sufficiency in foodstuffs was one of the avowed aims of both Fascism and National Socialism. Complete autarchy, on the other hand, has never been acknowledged to be among the aims of either régime. The numerous measures to replace imported raw materials by domestic substitutes have been the outcome not of ideological considerations, but of dire necessity and they were reluctantly embarked upon. The reason for this refusal of the leaders of the two countries to follow the wishes of the more extreme theorists is self-evident. The financial and economic mechanisms of our modern world so closely interlock that absolute autarchy is, practically, an impossibility. It could perhaps be made actual, but to do it would mean a tremendous sacrifice for everyone concerned. It could be done only at a high price in painful readjustments, accompanied by a general lowering of the standard of living, in a large country like the United States or the Soviet Union, each of which has a vast domestic market and almost unlimited supplies of virtually all raw materials. It would be nothing short of madness and suicide in countries such as Italy and Germany which depend on foreign markets and lack some, if not all, of the most essential raw materials.

The advocates of autarchy have been, I think, far more outspoken and persistent in Germany than in

Italy. But the Hitler Government could not over-
look the fact that even in 1931—that is, in the third
year of the depression—more than 36 per cent of
Germany's total industrial production was exported.
According to Dr. Wilhelm Röpke this meant that
almost 10 million Germans or about 15 per cent of
the entire population depended for their living upon
export trade. This may be the reason why the National Socialist Government has taken pains to indicate very clearly that it does not share the views of
autarchy's advocates. An official survey of economic
conditions and relations in Germany during 1933,
issued by the Ministry of Economics, says in part:
"Protectionism . . . has, in these last few years,
everywhere been spreading. If this continues it
must, necessarily, lead to growing economic isolation
among the nations and to an ever-increasing degree
of economic self-sufficiency. In the long run this
would mean the return to the primitive conditions
of bygone ages. This cannot be the aim of Germany
or of any other country whose interests lie in world
trade. For, in spite of tendencies to make countries
economically independent, it is generally realized
that modern facilities for transportation and trade
must be used to equalize the climate and geological
differences between continents and between countries, and bring about a closer spiritual cooperation
among the nations." Dr. Schacht has been a con-
sistent and untiring advocate of the liberalization of
international trade, although it became his painful
duty to devise and enforce some of the most rigid

import and export restrictions that have thus far been attempted by any country in time of peace. In his speech at the Leipzig Fair on March 4, 1935, Dr. Schacht declared that "National Socialism sees in orderly economic relations between nations an essential and indispensable cultural factor and is therefore ready and willing to cooperate in the restoration of world trade." This statement of the Minister of Economics and President of the Reichsbank was given wide publicity and may be held to represent the official policy of the National Socialist Government. Hitler gave this doctrine supreme unction in his speech of May 21, 1935, when he described "the idea of economic autarchy in any country" as "silly and its effect harmful to the Nation." The measures for economic self-sufficiency, therefore, which have, under duress, been taken by Italy and Germany cannot be rightly regarded as by-products of the ideology of the two movements but are merely, to repeat, the unhappy results of a situation that is beyond the control of the respective Governments.

ITALY'S FUNDAMENTAL WEAKNESS

Since the beginning of the East African war and the imposition of sanctions by the League of Nations the fundamental economic weakness of Italy has attracted so much attention that it seems almost superfluous to allude to it again. It is weakness growing out of Italy's dependence on imports for her fuel and her chief raw materials. She has to import practically the whole of her coal, oil, iron, steel, copper, lead, zinc, manganese ore, cotton and wool. She has no rubber, tin, nickel or chromium. In order to pay for these fuels and raw materials she must necessarily sell to foreign countries services and goods. The other two important items in Italy's balance of payments were tourist expenditures and emigrant remittances.

When a country is making fairly rapid progress toward industrialization but depends wholly upon the outside world for its essential supplies, one need not elaborate upon the vulnerability of its position. Italy's difficulties began even before the depression, and they originated, at least in part, in the overvaluation of the lira at the time of its stabilization in December 1927. In a notable speech at Pesaro on August 18, 1926, Mussolini laid down the basis of Italian monetary policy. "I will defend the lira to the last breath, to the last drop of blood," he declared. "I will never inflict on this splendid Italian people who have been working for the last four years under the most self-denying discipline, and who are prepared to make further and even heavier sacrifices, the moral shame and the economic calamity of the collapse of the lira." The Pesaro speech has been carved in stone and the Fascist Government has made truly heroic efforts to live up to the promise of the Duce. The maintenance of the lira at too high a level naturally tended to raise Italian prices, and thus weakened the competitive position of Italian industries in the world market. On the

other hand, the overvalued currency permitted Italy
to secure foreign raw materials at a lower real cost.
But the effect of overvaluation, on the whole, was
distinctly unfavorable to Italy's economic position.
The usual explanation of the high parity, in terms of
foreign exchanges, adopted in 1927, is that it was
due to considerations of national prestige. It will be
remembered that Great Britain had a somewhat
similar experience when in 1925 the pound sterling
was reestablished on a gold basis at too high a level.
But, while England after a bitter struggle was, in
September 1931, finally forced off the gold standard,
Italy refused to follow any such course. Even after
the outbreak of the East African campaign and the
ensuing international complications, the Fascist
Government continued to cling to the official gold
parity of the lira, although by the end of July 1935
the 40 per cent gold cover for notes in circulation
had been suspended. The reason for such a policy
was perhaps not merely the desire to live up to the
promise given by the Duce at Pesaro, and since
then many times reiterated, but also the need of
maintaining the confidence of investors in the stability of the domestic currency. For the Italian Treasury depends largely on the home market for the flo-
tation of government obligations made necessary
for the financing of budget deficits and programs of
public works.

The maintenance of a surplus from which the necessary raw materials could be paid for has been one
of the chief preoccupations of the Italian Govern-

ment. It led the Government to take a series of measures the purpose of which was, on the one hand, the fostering of Italian exports and, on the other, the cutting of imports to the bone. There was to be an elimination of everything not considered absolutely essential. The devaluation of the pound sterling and of currencies based on sterling in the early autumn of 1931 and, in its turn, the devaluation of the dollar in the spring of 1933 added further to the financial difficulties of Italy. It is true that devaluation cheapened raw materials purchased abroad with Italian currency and thus reduced the cost to the manufacturers. Moreover, the Treasury and certain private concerns derived a benefit from reduced interest charges on obligations payable in pounds and dollars. The volume of such obligations, however, was not great for Italy's foreign indebtedness has been kept at a notably low level. As over against these advantages, the depreciation of foreign currencies created new and formidable difficulties for Italian exports and it further intensified the evil effects of a depression that was accompanied by a catastrophic dwindling of international trade and a like decline in world prices. Members of the Italian Government and high officials of the Ministry of Finance never fail to point out that the depreciation of the pound and of the dollar constitute a factor of importance in this multiplication of Italy's difficulties. Many of them make it no secret that in their opinion the devaluation of the dollar and the subsequent repudiation by the United States Government of the gold-clause provision of its obligations were not the result of economic and financial necessities, but merely of amateurish experimentation with questionable economic theories. This opinion is, perhaps, not entirely devoid of foundation and is shared by a large number of economists and business men in this country.

Italian import trade declined from 21,665 million lire in 1929 to 7,667 million lire in 1934; the respective figures for exports are 15,236 million and 5,225 million. The unfavorable balance of trade was thus reduced from 6,429 million lire in 1929 to 2,441 millions in 1934. But this reduction in the deficit can hardly be considered an improvement since the ratio of imports to exports did not suffer any substantial change. For the first nine months of 1935 Italian imports amounted to 5,649 million lire and exports to, 3,681 million, which leaves an unfavorable balance of 1,968 million. Compared with the corresponding figures for 1934, imports declined by 21 million lire and exports by 140 million. Italian foreign trade during this period was dominated by military considerations, dictated by the East African expedition.

The two other important items in Italy's balance of payment—tourist expenditures and emigrant remittances—fared almost as badly. Under each of these headings Italy had a favorable balance of over 2,000 million lire in 1929. In 1932 the receipts from each of these sources is believed to have been reduced to less than half the figure for 1929.

Augsburg Seminary
Library

ITALY'S FINANCIAL AND TRADE POLICIES

These are the chief economic factors that determined the financial and commercial policies of the Fascist Government. And it must always be kept in mind that they developed against the background of an unparalleled world-wide depression. The two pillars of Italian financial policy were the "battle for the lira" and the balancing of the budget. Enough has been said of the former. Any inquiry into the budget situation presents great technical difficulties owing to the fact that the official figures for the various years are not, strictly speaking, comparable. Nevertheless the available computations indicate that from 1924–1925 to 1929–1930 the budget was balanced with the exception of the fiscal year 1927–1928, when there was a deficit of some 200 million lire. Beginning with 1930–1931 the situation grew worse, the budget could not be balanced and, in 1933–1934, the deficit reached the alarming figure of 6,458 million lire, an increase of 2,836 million over the deficit of the previous year. This great increase in the deficit of 1933–1934 is explained by the huge conversion operation undertaken by the Treasury in April 1934 at a considerable immediate cost to the Government. The general growth of the deficit resulted from the shrinkage of revenue due to the deterioration of business conditions and the program of public works embarked upon by the Government.

The desire to maintain Italy's export position without devaluing the lira led the Government to pursue a deflationary policy. Stern measures were taken to cut down costs. In December 1933 the official bank discount rate was reduced to 3 per cent, the lowest in the financial history of the Kingdom. Labor costs were stabilized at a low level through the operation of the collective contracts accompanied, as we have seen, by a substantial reduction in real wages. By a decree of November 18, 1930, all salaries and wages were reduced by a definite ratio which, in certain cases, was as much as 12 per cent. In April 1934 the operation was repeated and here the decreases were from 6 to 20 per cent, the higher percentage applying to the salaries of the members of the Government. By other edicts of the Government rents were twice reduced by 10 per cent, and once by 12. At the same time prices were cut in proportion to the reduction of earned incomes. This also was done by government decree. The measure was effectively enforced largely through the pressure brought upon commercial establishments by the Fascist organizations. The burden of taxation, according to Mussolini's own statement in the Chamber of Deputies on May 26, 1934, had reached its limit and could not be increased any further.

Deflationary policies had in Italy exactly the same effect as they have had in every other country. They brought with them unemployment and much hardship for a large number of people. This forced the Government to expand its program of public works and to use various employment-creating devices which were accompanied by a certain degree of credit inflation. The deflationary measures failing to improve Italy's export position, the Government had seen itself forced to follow a policy of restricting imports in order to preserve all available reserves of foreign exchange as sources of payment for necessary raw materials. Italy has been for many years a country with a high protective tariff. Nevertheless the Fascist Government showed great reluctance to use the most objectionable methods of protection, such as import and export licenses and quotas. And it was only in the end that it entered the path on which so many other countries had preceded it. Special legislation passed in 1933 empowered the Government to impose heavy surtaxes on commodities imported from countries which discriminated against Italy, especially through the application of quotas and licenses. In April 1934 import quotas were put into effect but only for articles on a restricted list. In the months that followed, however, the list was extended; and in April and June 1935 Italy's entire import trade was forced into the straitjacket of the most rigid of quota systems. Control over holdings of foreign securities and currency was also concentrated in the hands first of the Bank of Italy (December 1934) and, after May 1935 in those of the Superintendent of Foreign Exchanges, Professor Felice Guarneri. A decree of the Council of Ministers, issued in the midst of the military maneuvers at Bolzano on August 28, 1935, directed all Italians possessing foreign investments to turn them over to the Government in exchange for 5 per cent Italian

Treasury bonds. The same decree limited dividends to 6 per cent, the balance to be invested in government securities, and imposed a 10 per cent tax on all dividends, paid by Italian corporations. These were, of course, purely war measures.

The same desire to safeguard all available resources in order to be able to purchase essential raw materials led the Government to take a number of measures designed to diminish the use of certain commodities which could be replaced by domestic substitutes. Most important among them was a project providing for the development of electric power to take the place of coal, and other projects for the production of artificial fibre and synthetic gasoline. A decree of August 28, 1935, made the use of synthetic gasoline mandatory for all public vehicles after December 31, 1937. It is hardly necessary to add that all these measures have been difficult to enforce and very costly. They represent, no doubt, a distinct move toward autarchy, but a move which is the result of the depression and of the international situation, and not of the ideology of Fascism. The creation at the end of July 1935 of government monopolies for the purchase abroad of coal, tin, copper and nickel had the same purpose, that of eliminating unnecessary imports and of creating a "balanced" trade, i.e., the diverting of Italian orders to countries which would reciprocate by taking Italian goods. A similar intention inspired a number of "barter" agreements entered into by Italy with Poland, Turkey, Austria, Hungary, Germany and

Brazil. These agreements provided for a direct exchange of goods between the countries concerned, and it was hoped that they might help to a certain extent to mitigate the rigidity of export and import quotas.

This complex system of measures, which was not essentially different from that found in so many countries, was no more successful in Italy than it was anywhere else. The gold reserve of the Bank of Italy, which stood at 5,052 million lire in 1928, rose to 7,099 million in January 1934, but has steadily decline since. In January 1935 it had dropped to 5,822 million, and on October 20, 1935, reached a new low of 3,936 million. The decline was particularly rapid after July 23, 1935, when the minimum cover of 40 per cent was suspended. It is the avowed intention of the Government to sacrifice the gold reserve to the financing of the East African war. The internal debt increased between 1922 and 1935 by 31,295 million lire, and on January 31, 1935, showed a total of 105,004 million lire. Most of the new debt has been due to expenditures on public works and improvements of various kinds and has, therefore, gone to increase the nation's real assets. But it is by no means certain that all such investments can be classified as "productive"; and the burden that future generations will have to carry has also inevitably been increased. The Bank of Italy, on the other hand, has been successful in keeping down the volume of notes in circulation. It was reduced from 17,992 million lire in 1927 to 12,420 million in April

1934, and had increased only very slightly—to 12,787 million—on January 31, 1935. On August 20, 1935, the volume of notes in circulation stood at 13,707 million lire. There was a considerable revival in industrial production in this last year. The League of Nations index for Italy (1928=100) declined to 73 in 1932 but rose sharply to 88.3 in 1934 and to 102.1 in June 1935. This revival, which has already approached the dimensions of an industrial boom, was due entirely to government orders connected with the East African war.

All the efforts of Italy to maintain her trade and financial position have been brought to an abrupt end by the action taken in Geneva. Since the application of economic sanctions on November 18, 1935, and its possible extension to the most vital of Italian imports, the Rome Government has been confronted with problems of complete autarchy in its most unwelcome guise.

GERMANY'S POSITION

The financial and economic questions that Hitler had to face when he assumed power in January 1933 were, if somewhat different, certainly not less formidable than those that presented themselves to the attention of Mussolini. In Italy a much larger proportion of the population is engaged in agriculture than is the case in Germany, and the Italian peasants and workers have, to a much greater extent than have the Germans, retained the gift of being able to live on very little, sometimes on almost nothing, without being too unhappy. The one great consolation of always being poor is that one has nothing to lose.

Since 1933 Germany's financial and commercial policies have been determined by four major factors: dependence on foreign markets for the consumption of the exported products of her industry and also her ability to import some of the raw materials essential to her; increasing difficulties in obtaining foreign currencies; the huge internal and foreign debt inherited by the Third Reich from its predecessors and from the balmy era of extravagant international financing that ended so pitifully in 1929–1931; and the 6 million unemployed who contributed in no small degree to the success of the National Socialist movement and whom Hitler promised to put back to work.

I have already said that in 1931 more than 36 per cent of the total industrial production of Germany was exported. If this percentage has considerably declined since, this was not because but in spite of the efforts of the Government of the Reich. It is estimated that Germany depends on imported raw materials to the extent of 40 to 45 per cent of her entire consumption. In 1934, 58 per cent of her total imports consisted of raw materials. The cotton, jute, and silk industries depend entirely upon them. In 1934 the heavy industries and manufacturers of leather used imported raw materials to the extent of 60 per cent. For certain other important industries, such as margarine, beer and tobacco, the corresponding percentage was 35. About 90 per cent of Germany's raw wool and 95 per cent of her flax came from abroad. She has no rubber. In 1934, 32 per cent of her consumption of motor fuel and as much as 80 per cent of her consumption of gasoline were of foreign origin.

In order to pay for these imported raw materials Germany must necessarily export manufactured goods or those natural products that she possesses in surplus quantity, such as coal. But, since the depression her foreign trade has dwindled to less than one-third of what it was in 1928. In that year her imports amounted to 14,001 million marks and her exports to 12,276 million. In 1933 the respective figures were 4,204 million and 4,871 million, leaving a favorable balance of 667 million marks. In 1934 this balance was reversed. The imports increased to 4,451 million, and the exports declined to 4,167 million, producing a deficit of 284 million. The situation improved but slightly in the first six months of 1935. During this period the imports amount to 2,127 million marks and the exports to 1,962 million, leaving a deficit of 165 million.

Confronted with a trade balance that was becoming constantly more unfavorable, the Government entered upon a policy of reducing imports drastically and of promoting exports no less drastically. The reduction of imports has taken two different lines: a rigid control of all imports by special agencies and the giving of every encouragement to the production and use of such substitutes as can be used in place of materials formerly imported from abroad. The control of imports went through a number of preliminary stages and finally culminated in the introduction in September 1934 of the so-called "New Plan" which was the creation of Dr. Schacht. Under the "New Plan" 25 boards have been established, one for each of the chief imports; and only consignments of imports for which the boards have issued permits are allowed to enter. The granting of the import permit depends not only on the importance of the consignment itself but also on the available supply of foreign exchange. In spite of these rigid restrictions the balance of Germany's foreign trade, as we have seen, continued to be unfavorable during 1934 and in the first half of 1935. In August 1935, however, the trend was reversed. German imports were 318 million marks, while exports rose to 373 million; thus a surplus of 55 million marks resulted.

There is no way of knowing at the time of writing whether this trend is likely to continue. This, however, is not impossible, for the increase in the monthly volume of exports—the August 1935 figure is the highest since March 1934—may well be due to the effects of Dr. Schacht's "Export Subsidy Plan." The Export Subsidy Plan is the outcome of the Law of June 28, 1935, which bestowed on the Chamber of Economics the power to impose a levy on business firms and associations, the proceeds of which levy were to be used to finance exports and

put German exporters in a more favorable position
in the international market. Officially, the levy is
a "voluntary" one. That is, those who pay are
"voluntarily" making a contribution which will
keep Germany from being charged with dumping,
and which, at home, will remove any impression
that this levy is merely a new sales tax that the contributing firms and associations will simply pass
along to the consumer. It has not yet been stated
what amount can thus be placed in the hands of Dr.
Schacht, but it is believed that it will be something
between 720 and 1,000 million marks. And it means,
of course, the laying upon industry of a very heavy
burden.

The Government program for the cutting down of
imports likewise provides for first, the production
of various substitutes such as synthetic rubber, synthetic gasoline and artificial fibre (*Vistra*), and then,
second, for the giving of aid to the domestic development of branches of industry that have been neg-
lected in the past, such as the production of wool,
flax, lead, zinc and other raw materials usually imported from abroad. This program includes a variety
of measures. Among them are regulations for the
compulsory admixture of domestic raw materials—
for instance, the mixing of alcohol with gasoline;
premiums and subsidies; guaranteed prices, in the
case of wool, for instance, to encourage sheep breed-
ing; freedom from taxes on investments, with the
object of developing new branches of production;
and credits which the Government permits the Min-

istry of Finance to advance "for the forwarding of the domestic production of raw materials." There is also a complicated system of clearing agreements with various countries, and much encouragement is given to the promotion of foreign trade on a "barter" basis. The utmost that can be said in favor of these involved and often vexatious measures is that they have prevented foreign trade from expiring altogether. They certainly have done little to inject new life into it. The Germans themselves are under no illusions about it, and Dr. Schacht has spoken of his "New Plan" as a distasteful product of extreme emergency.

GERMANY'S FINANCIAL POLICIES

The unhappy condition of Germany's foreign trade, together with the drastic shrinkage of the "invisible" items of her balance of payments—tourist expenditures, shipping, insurance and banking—meant great difficulties in obtaining the foreign exchange necessary for the payment for essential raw materials and meeting the interest charges on Germany's foreign debt. The gold reserve of the Reichsbank had already been used by Hitler's predecessors to stop the gap left by the consistently adverse balance of payments. On December 31, 1928, the gold and foreign currencies reserve of the Reichsbank was 2,884 million marks. It had declined to 920 million on December 31, 1932, to 449 million on May 31, 1933, and to 136 million on May 31, 1934. During the first six months of 1935 the gold reserve was maintained at about 86 million marks and at the end of June it was 89 million.

Confronted with this situation and its inability to obtain foreign exchange, the Government resorted to the first of a series of measures that resulted in the declaration of a moratorium on the transfer of interest due on its foreign debt. The debt itself was not repudiated, but since then interest has been paid in German marks and only a small fraction of such currency payments is permitted to be transferred abroad. This suspension of transfers has, since July 1, 1934, been very nearly absolute. The transfer moratorium was brought about by the renewal and revision of the so-called "standstill agreements" which first came into effect in September 1931. The revisions were accompanied by fresh negotiations between the German Government and its foreign creditors, negotiations from which the unhappy creditors invariably emerged in a position worse than that in which they had found themselves before. One of the by-products of the agreements that led to the moratorium was the issue by Germany to its creditors of non-interest bearing scrip which, under certain complicated and involved conditions, could be used for financing German "additional exports." This method of financing "additional exports," first introduced in 1932, was originally directed against countries that obtained export advantages by depreciating their currencies and, since 1933, it had come more extensively into use. A second means of financing such exports was found in German bonds purchased on the foreign market and the so-called "blocked marks." Both scrip and blocked marks represent assets that cannot be transferred abroad but, under certain conditions, may be used to pay for exports from Germany. They can be obtained at a considerable discount. The whole procedure is one of extreme complexity and has led to much friction.

Through all her financial and economic difficulties Germany has steadily clung to a determination to maintain the mark at its gold parity. There has been much pressure from German exporters in favor of devaluation, but it has met with no response from the Government, especially since Dr. Schacht came to the Ministry of Economics in August 1934. At the end of the same month he spoke at Bad Eilsen, before the International Conference on Agricultural Science and delivered an address that attracted much attention. He argued strongly against devaluation, chiefly on the ground that practically the entire foreign debt of Germany had been contracted in terms of foreign currencies, and devaluation would therefore largely increase the debtor's burden. He also expressed the opinion that devaluation would not greatly help exporters, for German industry depended on imported raw materials, the cost of which would necessarily be increased. This would eventually lead to higher prices, a higher cost of living and higher wages. The lower value of the mark in terms of foreign currencies would also mean lower receipts from exports, and it was questionable whether this loss would be compensated for by an increase in the export volume. Dr. Schacht, moreover, argued that the general psychological effect of devaluation would be disastrous. He insisted on the necessity of a complete moratorium for several years, and the need of a drastic downward revision of Germany's debt structure, with a view to bringing it into keeping with the country's capacity to transfer.

The situation is paradoxical. The mark has no gold backing to speak of. Germany's financial weakness, internationally, is a fact of common knowledge. Yet the mark retains its official parity in terms of foreign exchange, although the various kinds of blocked marks are quoted at a considerable discount. At the same time currencies of nations such as Great Britain and the United States, whose financial and economic position is infinitely stronger than that of Germany, were subject to considerable fluctuations. The mystery is explainable in several ways. First of all is Germany's drastic curtailment of the service of foreign debt through the operation of transfer moratoria and the "standstill" agreements. Another important element is the absence of any currency inflation. The circulation of Reichsbank notes and other media of exchange has remained practically stable, fluctuating in narrow limits around 5,750 million marks. And lastly, the German Government has taken drastic measures to prevent the export of paper marks. This amounts to a virtual embargo and is rigidly enforced. All infractions of these regulations are punished by heavy fines and imprisonment. The system has worked thus far. But, Dr. Schacht's argument notwithstanding, it is probably detrimental to industry, which, moreover, is burdened with the heavy "export subsidy."

By the devaluation of the pound sterling, the dollar and other currencies, German exports have inevitably been affected adversely. But, on the other hand, public institutions and private concerns that had floated loans in terms of these foreign currencies greatly benefited by the devaluation. An estimate published in November 1935 by the Berlin Institute for Business Research indicates that to private administrative bodies alone the profit resulting from devaluation has amounted to some 1,900 million marks and that all private German debtors have benefited accordingly. As a result of the moratorium of transfers debtors were in a position to purchase their foreign bonds at a mere fraction of their face value. The total German foreign indebtedness, which stood at 23,200 million marks in February 1933 has since then greatly decreased. In May 1934 it was officially reported to have fallen to 17,900 million.

Any investigation of the present condition of the German budget is faced by practically insurmountable difficulties. A vital item in German public expenditures since 1933 has been the outlay for public works, various labor-creating devices, and armament. These expenditures are largely financed through the issue of "employment bills" which are short-term obligations but are renewable and are, for all practical purposes, long-term obligations. The "employment bills," moreover, are issued by various semi-official organizations disguised under innocuous names. The amount of such obligations has never been officially given out, and in the absence of definite information one has to rely on private computations. The London *Economist* estimated in June 1935 that the total internal debt of the Reich has increased, under the National Socialist régime, by between 12,000 and 16,000 million marks. This estimate is not very far from the total quoted to me in Berlin by well-informed persons. The Institute for Business Research in November 1935 took exception to such estimates and maintained that, at the end of June 1935 the entire public debt of Germany, including the Reich, the States and the municipalities, was 29,800 million marks. According to the same source the increase since the beginning of 1933 has been merely 4,340 million marks. The existence of a "secret" debt was specifically denied, and the total of the "employment bills" was given as some 5,000 million marks, of which about 1,000 million had already been funded. If the Institute for Business Research is right, the *Economist,* and also a great many authoritative German observers must be wrong. For, to repeat, the consensus of opinion in Berlin in the summer of 1935 was that the labor-creation program of the Government was financed by a surreptitious credit inflation on a scale that presented a very real danger to the financial position of the country.

It is unquestionable that the government policy of stimulating business and employment has had its effect. But what is doubtful is the soundness of the foundation on which this revival has been built up. Unemployment has been vastly reduced. The mark has been maintained at its official parity in spite of the absence of gold. For Germany the League of Nations index of industrial production (1928=100) has risen from 54 in 1932 to 80.9 in 1934, and in June 1935 stood at 95.2. Business has profited by the tax reduction program to the extent of 1,135 million marks, according to a statement made in September 1935 to the Nuremberg Congress of the National Socialist Party by Herr Reinhardt, Under Secretary of State for Finance. The Bureau of Statistics estimates that the national income has increased from 56,938 million marks in 1932 to 65,707 million in 1934. But there is also the other side of the picture. Foreign trade confined and hampered by the "New Plan," did not and cannot improve to any substantial degree so long as world conditions remain what they are. The foreign exchange situation is as bad as ever. The mark itself is maintained on a quasi-gold basis by methods which, if admittedly ingenious, are also objectionable and necessarily provisional.

The industrial revival that Germany experienced in 1935 was not due to normal causes. I have already quoted,[1] when discussing German unemployment, the interesting report of the Institute for Busi-

[1] See above, p. 144 *sqq*.

ness Research, which points out that the process of business recovery began in the middle of 1932 and that its progress since the autumn of 1934 and especially since the spring of 1935 was due largely to the Government's rearmament program. Both these admissions are of considerable interest, the first because it is in flagrant conflict with the official National Socialist theory that would credit the industrial revival entirely to the work of the Hitler Government. As a matter of fact, however, the upward trend had begun in Germany while she was still under the "Marxist-Liberal" régime, just as in the United States it started under President Hoover. But the fact that the present German revival has its source in the Government's rearmament program is far more important. It indicates how shifting and uncertain is the basis of this recovery. This conclusion is further reenforced by the statement of the Institute for Business Research that the revival that the consumption goods industries experienced in 1934 was due to "consumers' hoarding purchases" and to the increase in the number of marriages. Employment in these industries later suffered a setback from which it had not recovered by the autumn of 1935. The industries which at present show strong improvement are those engaged in manufacturing production goods, especially steel and iron, the metals in general, machines, vehicles, and optical instruments. The building trades have also been doing well.

But if rearmament is the real source of German

business recovery this does not augur well for public finances. The London *Economist* remarked in August 1935 that the reports of the Bureau of Statistics on rearmament finance "may be described as a private surmise complicated by official confusion." No wonder that so many financiers and business men in Berlin feel greatly worried and regard the future with much apprehension.

Dr. Schacht opened his address at the Leipzig Fair in March 1935 with the remark that "Economic policy is not a science but an art." And he went on to say that while the technique of every art can and must be learned, the creative power is something one must be born with. Dr. Schacht has undoubtedly a remarkable command of the technique of economics, and he has shown on more than one occasion that he has a real insight into the working of the intricate mechanics of economic forces. If, therefore, the structure of finance and international exchanges he has built up in Germany is rather an artifice than a work of art, it is the forces beyond the control of the Minister of Economics that should be blamed. Of the imperfection of his creation Dr. Schacht is, moreover, fully aware.

THE VERDICT

On a warm evening in the summer of 1935 I found myself on the terrace of a quaint casino of a small and little known German spa. It was at the end of a very busy day. I had motored in clouds of dust over

miles and miles of country roads and had visited
labor camps and peasant settlements, admired swimming pools and water works still in the process of
construction, and talked to a host of people, most
of them young officials of the present Government
who were eager to show me what they were doing.
After the somewhat bewildering and boisterous display of energy by this new Germany, I was ending
the day amid surroundings about as far removed
from all that as if I had entered a different world.
The buildings of the little old-fashioned spa went
back to the 1830's. Its elderly guests might still have
been living in pre-war days. Its orchestra was playing Schumann, Bach and Johann Strauss. Indeed,
the resort had for years been the favorite retreat of
the head of one of the dynasties that had been swept
away in the revolution of 1918. The place was still
full of memories of the old king. With me was a
pleasant young German, a government officer of the
new generation, jolly and athletic. Still in his early
twenties, he had grown up in the atmosphere of
National Socialism. He had fought the Führer's
battle on street corners and had now received his reward in the shape of an appointment as treasurer of
the local organization of the National Socialist
Party. He was full of the most exuberant enthusiasm and boundless devotion to the cause and he
was immensely proud of his uniform, his badges, the
importance of his office, his part in the Hitler movement. To my rather indiscreet question about the
condition of the finances of his organization, he ex-

claimed with his unfailing enthusiasm: *"Kolossal schlimm!"* ("Perfectly awful"). This verdict probably sums up the financial position of Germany and, since the beginning of the East African campaign, of Italy as well.

CHAPTER VIII

THE MAN IN THE STREET

THE BACKGROUND

IT is an old biblical truth that man does not live by bread alone. Fascism and National Socialism, as we have seen, are not oblivious of the fact while Dr. Ley is inclined to take it perhaps even too seriously. Propaganda in favor of the respective régimes and on a very large scale is carried on in both countries. But the Italian and German Governments have also taken numerous and effective steps for the betterment of many of the public services as a part of their extensive programs of public works. The resulting improvements receive wide publicity, which is occasionally more than their legitimate due, and the prestige of the government is accordingly enhanced. Any visitor who returns to Italy after an absence of several years cannot but be struck by the great changes that have taken place in both the physical equipment of the country and the attitude of the people with whom he has to deal in the ordinary business of life. There are many new and very good roads, a large number of new libraries, schools and other public buildings. The railroad service has been vastly improved. Trains run according to schedule, something they rarely did before; luggage is no longer tampered with in transit and arrives safely at its destination. The electrification of many of the lines has added greatly to the comfort of the traveller. There are many good, new athletic fields and stadiums, of which the truly magnificent Forum Mussolini in Rome is the most shining example. The seashore and the mountains are dotted with innumerable camps and summer colonies where a great proportion of young Italians and not a few of the older generation get an opportunity to forget their daily toil. For many of the children who come from the crowded tenements of the industrial cities these weeks in the country, made possible by the Fascist Government, are a real revelation. There is an unmistakable change in the attitude of the people themselves. Railway porters and taxi drivers are much more moderate and far less insistent in their demands for extra remuneration, and not infrequently forgo it altogether, which is a welcome change from an old tradition. Tips in the hotels are officially prohibited, and although they are expected and gratefully received they are no longer a source of unpleasantness. The dignity of labor is not merely a phrase in Fascist Italy.

It is the Eternal City that has undergone the most remarkable transformation. Until the East African venture the chief practical manifestation of Fascism's glorification of the Roman tradition took the form of extensive archæological excavations in the capital. In the course of this work many familiar landmarks disappeared in order that remnants of the

days of the Cæsars might be uncovered. Entire
sections of the city have gone and have given place
to new and magnificent avenues such as the Via
dell'Impero, the Via dei Trionfi and the Via del
Circo Massimo. They provide appropriate settings
for the parades of the black-shirted legions. Much
of this new Roma Mussoliniana is truly admirable,
but the cramped and swarming lanes that are no
longer there will be missed by many of Rome's old
friends. The fact that in the past the reputation of
this quarter was not of the best may seem to some
to be rather cold comfort. Rome has today one of
the best and most efficient bus services in the world,
and the skill with which the drivers pilot their heavy
vehicles through narrow and tortuous streets, where
one would hardly dare to venture in a Ford, is truly
amazing. More than that, Rome is now a remark-
ably clean city, the streets being washed four times
a day, which certainly was not the case in the past.
Mussolini has endowed the capital with its own
bathing beach, Ostia, which can be reached in 20 or
30 minutes, either by car or electric train. It is
widely used in the summer by business people, who
take advantage of the traditionally long midday
closing of offices to spend a couple of hours in the
sunshine. For many Romans the customary siesta
and hours in the *osteria* are a thing of the past,
which in itself gives Fascism an excellent claim to
having accomplished a revolution. There are perhaps too many glaring lights in the evening and, unfortunately, Roman nights have not been able to

escape the deplorable and vulgar practice of search-
light illuminations of public buildings and monuments. This makes it practically impossible, until
the searchlights have been mercifully turned off at
midnight, to get away from the gleaming lines of
the huge memorial to Vittorio Emanuele, a memorial that surely adds little to the beauty of the Eternal City. This present-day Roma Mussoliniana is
different from the Rome of fifteen years ago. It is
symbolic of the Fascist régime. It is more sanitary,
more efficient, brighter and bolder than it used to
be. But something of the refinement and charm of
the old Rome has been lost in the process of mod-
ernization.

Germany, naturally, did not undergo any such
striking change. Her trains, since time immemorial,
have run on schedule, her baggage cars have been as
safe as the vaults of a bank, and her railroad and
hotel employees have always been efficient, courteous and scrupulously honest. Her air service, which
is one of the best in the world, was a creation of
Hitler's predecessors. But there are many excellent
new motor roads under construction, athletic
grounds and swimming pools. The number of camps
and summer colonies for young and old has vastly
increased under the National Socialist régime. In
1935 Berlin was in no way different from what it
had been in 1932, except that one saw a great many
more men in brown S. A. and black S. S. uniforms.
As in the past, everything was spotless, orderly and
peaceful. In the midst of the feverish building and

decorating activities of the summer season the darkened and deserted Reichstag building in the Tiergarten spoke silently but eloquently of the passing of an era. In the square in front of it Bismarck and Moltke in bronze impassively gaze upon the rising of a new Reich, so different from the one they helped to build.

THE NEW WAY

But if, on the surface, Germany is not very different from what it was before the appearance of the Third Reich, the gradual transformation of social habits and the social structure is perhaps even more far-reaching than it is in Italy. Fascism and National Socialism, we know already, have been particularly active in bringing people into their fold in ever-increasing numbers, an object so largely achieved through the activities of the *Dopolavoro* and the *Kraft durch Freude,* of the various youth organizations—the *Balilla, Avanguardisti* and *Hitler Jugend*—and of the many other organizations controlled by the Fascist and the National Socialist Parties. The paternal hand of the Rome Government reaches forth to those Italians who live beyond the seas. In the summer of 1935 special camps and summer colonies were maintained for the children of Italian emigrants, who were brought back to the mother country from every corner of the world. These children received an enthusiastic and affectionate welcome such as they are not likely to forget. The money spent by the Government in these days of deserted ocean liners and subsidized shipping was no tremendous sum, and the effect of this home-coming on the minds of the young expatriates will probably be a lasting one.

Extremely important, I think, is another transformation, that which old methods of carrying on social and relief work have undergone. Great pains have been taken, especially in Germany, to make aid of this kind more personal and less coldly formal, even though the amounts distributed have not necessarily increased. The Fascist and the National Socialist Parties have taken over all existing relief and welfare organizations and set up a number of new ones. Through these agencies the local organs of the Parties carry on the work of their predecessors in the name of the respective Parties and often in the name of Mussolini and Hitler. It is strongly emphasized that relief is not a charity, but the right of the recipient and, correspondingly, one of the duties of the community. The principle itself is, of course, by no means novel; it is the very basis of unemployment insurance. The chief German agency for relief is the *Volkswohlfahrt* which existed in pre-Hitler days. It now has millions of members and has done excellent work. The Winter Relief (*Winterhilfe*) is an innovation of the National Socialist régime. It brings its aid to the needy with the slogan "Fight Hunger and Cold." The necessary funds are provided by widely advertised public campaigns accompanied by sales of lottery tickets, pamphlets, flowers, tags, medals and ribbons. Every first Sunday during the winter months each German family is expected to eat just a single meal, consisting of only one course cooked in one pot. The cost per each member of the family must not be more than some very small specified sum. The difference in cost between this frugal meal and the normal dinner is given to the fund for Winter Relief. The act is a "voluntary" one, but it is something that everybody does. I have already quoted Hitler's statement at the opening of the Winter Relief campaign of 1934 in which he strongly emphasized the ideological and social importance of this method of letting those who have shared with those who have not. A special day is set aside every year for a drive for Winter Relief funds. It is known as the "Day of National Solidarity" (*Tag der nationalen Solidarität*). In 1934–1935 the Winter Relief obtained 362 million marks and, in various ways, was able to help some 13.5 million people. These commendable activities have aspects that are somewhat reminiscent of the methods of Tammany Hall, although I was assured by observers generally critical of National Socialism that political differences are not permitted to interfere with the relief of the needy.

Highly significant, too, is the kind of rough and ready comradeship that is consistently cultivated in the Fascist and National Socialist organizations, without any interference, of course, with the principles of discipline and hierarchy. The members of the Fascist Militia and of the National Socialist

S. A. and S. S. are drawn from every level of society, but there are no social distinctions under either black shirt or brown, just as there are none under the uniforms of army privates. In Rome during the imposing State funeral of Luigi Razza and his companions who, in August of 1935, perished in an aeroplane accident on their way to East Africa, I watched the Fascist Militia which lined the streets along which the funeral procession moved. The militiamen were obviously a cross-section of today's Italy. Many were unmistakably peasants and workers. But not a few came obviously from the bourgeois circles and some were wearing the monocle. It is the rule among the members of the same troop of the S. A. to address each other by the familiar *"du"* instead of the formal *"sie."* On the several tours I took in the company of National Socialist officials our drivers, who were usually in the uniform of the S. A. or the S. S., invariably shared our meals, and not infrequently joined freely in our talk. As the social and economic structure of the two countries is still very much what it was before, such intimacy with "their betters" cannot but be pleasant and even flattering to men who are in more humble circumstances.

In this respect, as in many others, National Socialism has gone farther than Fascism. The classlessness of the Third Reich has found its practical expression in the Labor Service (*Arbeitsdienst*). It began as a voluntary organization in connection with the relief of unemployment and, looked at in that way, it is not vastly different from the Civil Conservation Corps of the United States. But the Labor Service is much more than a relief measure. With every justification it may be regarded as the preliminary stage of military training. Above all, it is the embodiment of the principle laid down by Hitler on May 1, 1933, that it is the duty of every German to do manual work, at least for a short time. Service with the labor corps was made obligatory first for university undergraduates and then made a necessary requirement for men entering government employment. Since October 1, 1935, it has been compulsory for all young Germans. The term of service is six months. A similar service exists for women, but so far it is on a voluntary basis. But for women, too, the Chancellor expressed his intention of some time making such work compulsory. The purpose of the Labor Service is to give practical training in "national solidarity," accompanied by hard physical labor and a large dose of National Socialist ideology. The young men are doing non-competitive work, such as land improvement, the draining of marshes, highway construction and the like. They are given a thorough preliminary military training, wear uniforms, and live in camps and barracks under conditions of Spartan simplicity. I visited several of these camps in various parts of Germany in 1934 and 1935, and I must admit that I was impressed by not only the truly German perfection of the organization, but also by the healthy and cheerful appearance of the young men themselves and the obvious pride they took in their hard physical labor. The *Arbeitspflicht* is very much in the foreground of the German picture today. At the great National Socialist demonstration in Berlin's Tempelhof on June 29, 1935, the gray-green columns of the labor battalions, wearing their characteristic caps, and carrying shovels instead of rifles, marched with the precision of the old Prussian regiments of the guards. They received a great ovation.

THE ROMANTIC ELEMENT

Appeal to the emotions plays an important part in the technique of both Fascism and National Socialism. Rome and Berlin each have their own Ministry of Propaganda. Count Ciano, Mussolini's son-in-law, presides over the one, and Dr. Goebbels over the other. The family relationship between the Italian Minister of Propaganda and the Duce has won for his department the nickname of the Ministry *sui generis*. While there is nothing these Ministries of Propaganda could teach the expert managers of political campaigns in democratic countries, there is that all-important distinction between the two cases that no counter-propaganda is permitted in either Italy or Germany. Fascism and National Socialism are assuming more and more the character of religions. I have already discussed their theology. They have their prophets, their saints and their martyrs, their rites and their symbols. The high priests and prophets of the new cults are, of course, Mussolini

and Hitler. The effigies and pictures of the Duce
and the Führer, on foot, on horseback, in aeroplanes
and on board ship, inspecting troops, receiving the
first offerings of the new harvest, visiting farms, or
kissing children are to be seen everywhere, and are
displayed quite as prominently as the Blue Eagle
used to be in the United States in the palmy and
now defunct days of the New Deal. Both the Fascist
and the National Socialist Parties publish official
synodics containing the names of men who have
fallen for the cause. The central and local headquarters of both Parties often have memorial halls. On
their walls, amidst banners of the various Party organizations surrounding the bust or portrait of the
Duce or the Führer, may be seen tablets commemo-
rating the heroes of the movement. The lictor's rods
or the swastika are, of course, to be seen everywhere. That spirit of comradeship I have already
mentioned is extended by the Fascists and the National Socialists to the men who had fallen in the
struggle for the cause. During the funeral of Razza
and his companions in Rome I witnessed the performance of the "Fascist Rite." The cortege halted
in the Piazza dei Cinquecento. The Secretary of the
Party stepped forward and, one by one, he called
the dead by name. As each name rang out the assembled multitude answered as one man: *"Presente."*
It would be idle to deny that even to a complete
unbeliever the ceremony was deeply moving. The
same ritual was followed in Munich in November
1935 when the remains of the sixteen who perished

in the abortive *Putsch* of 1923 were solemnly transferred to their new resting place in the centre of a
new and imposing group of buildings that house the
activities of the National Socialist Party. "The ceremony was replete with that symbolism so dear to
the German heart," wrote F. T. Birchall, the distinguished correspondent of the *New York Times,* "and
it was extremely impressive." On this occasion the
Führer followed the same route he had taken twelve
years ago, the route that had led his companions to
their death and had ended for him in his trial and a
prison term at Landsberg. Moreover, even as twelve
years ago, the column was led by Julius Streicher,
Hitler following as one of the rank and file. The
symbolic pageantry of this and similar occasions has
reached in Italy, and especially in Germany, a degree of perfection for which a parallel is hardly to
be found in democratic countries.

Fascist and National Socialist usages have gradually worked their way into the routine business of
life. The Roman salute is not very frequently seen
in Italy, but the Hitler salute is for all Germans
practically compulsory. Every official and many private letters now end with the familiar *"Heil Hitler!"*
The Hitler salute, as taught in the labor camps, the
S. S. and the youth organizations, is really more
than an ordinary greeting. It is quite a little ceremony which requires the assumption of a rigid
stance, heel clickings, the raising of the hand and
then the enunciation of the sacred formula. I had a
distinct feeling that the younger men took no small

pleasure in the performance. It is difficult to see
how they could lose the habit.

What is even more important perhaps is that this
Fascist and National Socialist romanticism extends
likewise to ways of thinking. When one begins to
consider current problems in terms of the Roman
tradition or of the muddled ideology of National
Socialism one may easily reach the most unexpected
conclusions, especially when currents of free ideas
and independent thought are completely shut off
through a rigid control over the press. The Italian
Fascists are bent on the complete and final extermination of the *dolce far niente* and dream of turning
the Neapolitans and Sicilians into effective and relentless "producers." With many other friends of
Italy I sincerely hope that they will never succeed
in this purpose. In Germany the "spiritual revolution" went a great deal farther. On one occasion I
visited the school for the leaders of the Labor Service, which occupies one of the wings of the palace
at Potsdam. The officer who took me about explained to me that under the "Marxist-Liberal"
régime the building that today houses this school
was once occupied by Isadora Duncan and her pu-
pils. So unseemly a desecration of the temple has
been piously obliterated by the National Socialists.
They have resanctified the temple by turning it over
to the Labor Service and have thus restored it to
the traditions of Frederick the Great. The officer
was most earnest about it. One of my German
friends of long standing, who has recently been con-

verted to the tenets of National Socialism, tried to persuade me that there was no compulsory military service in Germany today, and that service in the army was merely a moral duty. He admitted that the non-fulfillment of this duty was bound to have immediate and unpleasant consequences, but his answer was the startling argument that a man who was not doing his duty was not a worthy member of the community. Indeed he described this as a striking manifestation of Germany's "spiritual revolution." Such reasoning was particularly puzzling, because it came from a former Prussian officer with a good practical knowledge of the world. On another occasion I had to listen to an involved argument in defense of the hereditary farm law. The indivisibility of landed estates in pre-revolutionary Prussia, I was told, had rendered inestimable service to Germany. Under this arrangement the elder son became the squire, the second went into the army and became an officer, and the third was supposed to take holy orders. The hereditary farm law would benefit National Socialist Germany along the same lines. One son, whether the eldest or the youngest, would carry on the work on the farm, and the second would provide suitable material for the corps of non-commissioned officers. What was to happen to the other sons remained somewhat uncertain. Surely they could not all be turned into minor dignitaries of the church! One more example. The owner of a large estate in Brandenburg gave me a very detailed exposition of his interpretation of the *Weltanschauung*.

It was utterly impossible for me to agree with his ideas, but, considering that I had provoked the discussion, I tried to find a way out by making what I thought was a conciliatory remark to the effect that the economic policies of National Socialism had many elements in common with those of the New Deal. My inspiration proved to be an unhappy one. Indeed, it provoked a real explosion, and I was told rather sharply that the two policies could in no sense be compared, for Hitler was a man who had both high ideals and a keen sense of reality, while the first of these elements was entirely lacking in the President of the United States. National Socialism, indeed, is living in a world of its own. The intellectual atmosphere of Fascist and National Socialist circles partakes of that of the barracks, the Y. M. C. A. and a religious revival meeting. The proportion of these ingredients varies from case to case. It depends to a certain extent on the most recent instructions from the Party, but chiefly on the person to whom one happens to be talking and also, perhaps, on the particular mood of that person at the time. Although found in both Italy and Germany, it is in Germany that it is particularly pronounced.

If we turn to the probable evolution of Fascism and National Socialism—presuming, of course, that they will survive for a number of years—two important elements must be kept in mind. The first is that each of the two movements has absorbed many men and women who were formerly in opposition, including even Communists. The second, which is more significant, is that the Fascist and the National Socialist Parties have been for some time closed associations and that they take no new members except those who graduate from the youth organizations. At the end of 1934 the Fascist Party had some 1,850,000 members. The membership of the National Socialist Party is larger, perhaps twice as large. The road into the Party is practically free and, indeed, almost inescapable for those young people who have received the proper schooling. Such recruits necessarily come largely from the lower levels of society, for in them of course are found the great mass of humanity. How the resultant and inevitable change in the social complexion of the membership of the Fascist and of the National Socialist Parties will eventually affect their future course it is impossible to say at present. But I think that the outlook offers little ground for the rather common belief that Dr. Schacht and his friends are firmly in control of Germany's destiny. This seems to be true today, but it is by no means impossible that the real Fascist and National Socialist revolutions are merely beginning.

THE STEP-CHILDREN

The population of Italy and Germany does not consist of either Fascists or National Socialists alone. Even Dr. Goebbels was willing to admit this when, commenting on the assertion that all Germans today are National Socialists, he remarked in June 1935 that "we hope this is true, but we do not believe it is true." The fate of the outspoken opponents of the two régimes is so well known that it hardly needs elaboration. Communists, Socialists, Liberals, all those who took an active part in the struggle against Fascism and National Socialism or were suspected of being hostile have been subjected to great brutality and indignities. Some lost their lives. Many more went to prison. Thousands went into the *confino* on the Italian islands or into the German concentration camps, where their fate under the supervision of black-coated guards is of the bleakest. Tens of thousands fled the country, to swell the ranks of the army of political refugees, an army that has grown to alarming dimensions since the war of 1914–1918, which was fought by the Allies and the United States in the name of political freedom and democracy, was brought to a successful end. None of these facts is denied in either Italy or Germany, but they are usually dismissed with the remark that a revolution is a revolution. Tragic and deplorable as are these persecutions of men and women whose crime, in an overwhelming number of cases, consists merely in disagreeing with the opinions of the new rulers, they are nevertheless not the worse side of the picture. It is true that they are persecutions which have deprived Italy and Germany of many of their leaders in the fields of science, art, literature and public life. But of still greater consequence is the régime of complete sup-

pression of any freedom of thought that has been
rigidly enforced by Fascism and National Socialism.
The press, literature, the universities and schools,
indeed, all things that cannot grow in the absence of
intellectual freedom have been submitted to the
most ruthless regimentation. Italian and German
universities today are like cenotaphs or empty
mausoleums. The technical branches have suffered
less, and the dismissal of some of their eminent professors was the chief loss. Good and even excellent
work is still being done in medicine, mathematics,
chemistry, engineering and other "non-political"
sciences. But the position of the humanities is truly
and deeply tragic. History, law, economics and
philosophy have to be taught in the spirit of Fascism
and National Socialism. Some professors still succeed in defeating the strictness of regulations making use of this subterfuge or that, but their position
is precarious, and it is all humiliating to the last
degree. The atmosphere of the universities has also
changed. Nothing is left of the traditional liberalism
and earnest search for truth for which these ancient
Italian and German seats of learning were so rightly
famous throughout the centuries. Politics have in-
vaded them. The bulletin boards of Italian and
German universities are covered with propagandist
posters, and in Germany the violently anti-Semitic
publication *Der Stürmer* is frequently displayed in
the place of honor. The old German student corporations, with their quaint uniforms and, if you like,
with their foolish traditions, had either to disband or

to bow to the commands of the National Socialist Party. Service in the labor corps is a necessary qualification for an academic position, and membership in the S. A. or S. S. is also a requirement which, if not official, is nevertheless unescapable.

Even the appearance of the universities has changed. Everywhere are the lictor's rods or the swastika, even on the seal of the Economics Seminar of the University of Berlin. There is gloom, fear and foreboding among the many who teach and have no sympathy with the Hitler movement. The University of Berlin has long been in the habit of honoring its distinguished teachers by placing their busts in the hall of the main building. Some of them are gone now, and no one seems to know whether the disappearance of this bust or that can be traced to a need of cleaning or repair, or to the discovery by some zealous National Socialist investigator that the views or the ancestry of the distinguished scholar do not justify the honor under the new régime.

The position of the press is, if possible, even more tragic. It has simply to write or print under orders, and even its selection of news, whether domestic or foreign, must pass scrutiny by the appropriate Italian or German officials. Little wonder that Italian and German papers are hopelessly dull, and that foreign papers are eagerly sought. Chauvinistic, narrow, and thoroughly objectionable newspapers exist in every country, and some of them have a wide circulation and a great following. Not a few, indeed, may stand comparison with the newspapers of present-day Italy and Germany. But where there is freedom of the press no one need read them unless he so chooses. In Fascist Italy and National Socialist Germany the most fundamental and undeniable right of every man—the right to think, say and write what he believes to be true—is completely and relentlessly denied. The apostles of Fascism and National Socialism have not yet learned and probably will never learn the simple fact that we cannot arrive at absolute truth, and that the only road that leads in that direction is the road of conflicting and freely expressed opinion. But for such theories, of course, there is no room in an ideology that preaches faith, discipline and obedience.

CONFLICT WITH THE CHURCH

The attitude of the National Socialist Government toward the Church has attracted much attention abroad, and has aroused a possibly general indignation. Mussolini had his own violent struggle with the Holy See. In his early days the Duce was not only furiously anti-clerical, but also anti-Christian. The expulsion of the Pope from Rome was openly advocated by some Fascists in 1919. But times have changed. In 1929 the Roman question was brought to an end by the Lateran Treaty, and

at the same time Italy and the Vatican put their
signatures to a Concordat. A great deal of friction,
however, developed when it was put into force and
on more than one occasion the relations between the
Pope and the Duce were strained almost to the
breaking point. What caused the conflict was, substantially, the same thing that produced similar
trouble in Germany a few years later: the refusal of
the totalitarian State to admit the Church's right to
control organizations of young people. The Italian
dispute with the Vatican was brought to a compro-
mise solution in the early autumn of 1931. The
Catholic organizations of young people were permitted to continue, but their activities were so drastically curtailed that they no longer interfered with
the supremacy of the State. These organizations
were specifically enjoined from carrying on any
sports or athletic activities. The Church question in
Italy was somewhat less complex than in Germany
because virtually all Italians are Roman Catholics,
and the Catholic Church itself is a highly centralized institution. In spite of its international character the Vatican is under strong Italian influence
and is united with the Italian State by close and
numerous ties. All this, perhaps, played its part in
smoothing out the conflict between the Duce and
the Holy See.

The religious problem in Germany is a great deal
more involved owing to the variety of Germany's
religious denominations. Von Papen's success, when

in the name of the Hitler Government he was able
to conclude a Concordat with Rome, was largely
offset by the difficulty of carrying it into effect. The
chief reason, as noted above, was the same as that
in Italy, the refusal of the State to permit any organizations of young people to be under the control
of the Church. In Germany, moreover, there was a
long series of conflicts between the State and the
different religious denominations, which likewise
grew out of the determination of the Hitler Government to prevent any interference from religious
bodies in what it considered to be the rightful
sphere of State activity. As to what constitutes the
precise limits of this sphere, that is something which
the Government, of course, reserves the right to determine for itself. More oil was thrown upon the
fire by the extravagant attacks upon Christianity
indulged in by some of the National leaders and
their attempts to create a new religion based on the
worship of Teutonic heroes. The conflict between
Church and State led to the summary removal and
to the arrest and prosecution of a number of distinguished churchmen. I shall not attempt to review the various phases of this dark chapter in
Germany's history, which is still by no means closed.
It will suffice to point out that, although freedom of
faith is openly proclaimed by National Socialism, it
is subjected in practice to treatment which is essentially the same as that meted out to all individual
liberty in the totalitarian State.

THE JEWISH QUESTION

We have already seen that the Fascist doctrine of the Nation is not based on any concept of race and that therefore, fortunately for Italy, the teachings of Mussolini are free from anti-Semitism. No other phase of the German situation has so shocked the conscience of the world as has National Socialism's militant and intolerant policy toward the Jews. Germans are constantly pointing to and stressing the fact that race discrimination and anti-Semitism are by no means German inventions. This is unfortunately only too true. Discrimination against the Negroes in the United States, and the complete exclusion of Orientals from immigration by Act of Congress are familiar instances. They find their fitting counterparts in the legislation and practice of a number of countries. Anti-Semitism and social discrimination against the Jews are also unhappily far from being merely a product of National Socialism. But there is a wide abyss between social discrimination and a policy that practically aims at the extermination of a whole section of the population, although it must be admitted that the unwritten but *absolute* rule of at least one New York club which bars all Jews from membership offers food for sad reflection, especially since the club in question counts among its members representatives not only of the social but also of the intellectual *élite* of the country. These considerations in no way justify the National Socialist policy. Restrictions on immigration cannot properly be compared with the measures taken by the Hitler Government against the Jews. Many such restrictions may be criticized on good ground as unsound and objectionable. But the difference between the two cases is clear and striking. It is one thing to prevent foreign settlers from coming into the country; it is something very different practically to make outcasts of a whole group of one's fellow citizens.

Anti-Semitism was one of the first tenets of National Socialism. It was an article of the original program, and it is indoctrinated with extraordinary violence by Hitler in *Mein Kampf*. The National Socialist Government has practised it with systematic and relentless persistence. Beginning on April 1, 1933, with the one-day boycott of shops and stores owned by the Jews, the persecution has gone steadily on. Under the so-called Nuremberg Law, enacted in September 1935, the Jew in Germany has been condemned to an all but absolute exclusion from every trade and profession and to a complete segregation as well. With a perverted logic and perseverance that is maniacal, National Socialism has likewise extended its restrictive and deadly edicts not only to Jews, but also to all persons having a specified percentage of Jewish blood in their veins. I shall not try to follow the Nuremberg legislators in their experiment in this sinister race alchemy. The position of the Jews in Germany today is perfectly clear: it is wholly intolerable. To add to the legal restrictions, which were designed to prevent them from earning a living and which have largely succeeded in their purpose, Germany's Jews are subject almost daily to violent attacks from the leading figures of National Socialism, among whom Goebbels, Streicher and Rosenberg have particularly distinguished themselves. It would serve no useful purpose if I cited instances of their gross and vulgar abuse which have been fully reported in the press. To make things worse, even emigration has been made difficult and extremely costly by stringent restrictions on the transfer abroad of German funds —though, for that matter, many of the Jews have nothing to transfer.

A very puzzling aspect of the situation is that the persecution of the Jews continues relentlessly in spite of the fact that it is not popular with a section of even National Socialist opinion. I know personally of a case where a firm engaged in a business from which Jews are definitely barred, continues to employ one of them. The head of the firm is a member of the Party and an S. S. man; practically his whole staff, with the exception of the Jewish employee, are also members of various National Socialist organizations. Discovery by the authorities of the presence of that forbidden employee would certainly have most serious consequences for the firm in question and especially for its head. He nevertheless takes the risk on the ground that he cannot throw into the street a man who has been in his employ for years and has shown himself to be a useful and a faithful co-worker.

Even more puzzling, perhaps, is the attitude of some of Hitler's warmest admirers who completely disagree with his anti-Jewish policies. By chance I met in Berlin a man I had known many years before, under an entirely different sky. He is quiet, middle-aged, of good education, and has had a good deal of experience of the world. He surprised me by the statement that he had recently joined the S. A. And he surprised me even more when he spoke of Hitler as the greatest man not only in Germany but in the world. I asked about the Jewish question, which was much in the public mind at the time, as a result of violent anti-Jewish outbursts on Kurfürstendamm, outbursts, indeed, which had a distinct flavor of the old Russian pogroms. He said that the whole thing was perfectly disgusting, but that Hitler was in no way responsible for it. And he advanced the quite fantastic theory that the anti-Jewish policy was carried on largely against the will of the Führer by the high officials of the Party, who were under the influence of Baltic Germans from the former provinces of Russia. These Baltic Germans, among whom is Rosenberg, had brought with them to Germany their violent anti-Semitism; and it has been made even more violent as a result of the Soviet Revolution, which is usually interpreted in reactionary Russian circles as having been made possible by the Jews. My natural question was whether he had read *Mein Kampf*. He said he had and it was a marvellous book, but that Hitler was nevertheless not really opposed to the Jews. How the two things can go together is, for me, still a mystery. This conversation, however, took place before the passing of the Nuremberg laws.

The anti-Jewish policy of National Socialism has harmed Germany more in the outside world than has any other measure of the Hitler Government. Everyone probably knows people who speak rather sympathetically of Mussolini, but bitterly denounce Hitler. And it is very common, especially among a certain type of so-called radicals, most violently to abuse both Mussolini and Hitler for their trampling down of all freedom and at the same time to praise highly the Soviet Union, although Moscow shows even less respect for the bourgeois principle of individual freedom than does Rome or Berlin. But in the persecution of people on the ground of race there is something that is particularly shocking. It seems to be a distinct return to the darkest days of the Middle Ages; and coming as it does from a country of Germany's cultural standing and traditions it is something to which one finds it impossible to become reconciled.

The very worst feature of this unhappy situation is that there is, apparently, no way out. Anti-Semitism permeates the entire structure of Germany to such an extent that it is hopeless to expect

that it can be abandoned. Assuming that National
Socialism will continue to maintain its power, the
only solution of the Jewish question one can suggest is that, by degrees, Germany's Jews may drift
away to other countries. But this is hardly any solution at all.

DEMOCRACY VS. THE TOTALITARIAN STATE

The position of the ordinary citizen in the totalitarian State is not exactly an easy one. If he is fortunate enough to be carried away by the eloquence
of its leaders and to come to believe in the principles of Fascism and National Socialism, he may
derive no small satisfaction from participating in
the manifold activities of the State and of the
Party. But if he cannot let himself be so carried
away he finds himself in the position of a hostage
in an enemy camp. Theory and practice in the case
of both Fascism and National Socialism find themselves in hopeless contradiction. The theory speaks
of free and voluntary cooperation for the great common purpose, of the supremacy of the interests of
the Nation over the interests of the individual. In
practice, however, these high-sounding phrases are
reduced to the code of the ruthless martinet, complete distrust of everyone who does not belong to
the chosen few, and oligarchical rule by a self-
appointed *élite*. There is no freedom of opinion, no
freedom of the press, no recognized opposition. It

is probably true that both Italy and Germany have succeeded in achieving a considerable degree of national unity. But the sacrifices they have had to make in the process have assuredly been heavy.

The two régimes, moreover, give one the peculiar feeling that they are alike strong, and at the same time fragile. Their strength resides in the fact that they have succeeded in enrolling so many people under their banners and in identifying themselves with the routine of life and immediate interests of a very large number of their followers. Their chief weakness, as forms of government, consists not only in the danger inherent in all political suppression, which is bound to breed discontent, but also in the fact that they are eminently personal régimes. Fascism is identified with Mussolini and National Socialism with Hitler. It is difficult to imagine what will happen when the leaders are gone. Personal dictatorship necessarily makes it difficult to prepare a successor, lest in the end he become a rival. That process of selection which is possible in a democracy is totally lacking under Fascism and National Socialism. On the other hand, it must be remembered that Lenin likewise towered high above his followers, but that nevertheless at his death he was succeeded by Stalin who, little known as he was at the time, has been at the helm ever since. Government by a dictatorial Party organization may acquire such strength that its self-perpetuation may become a practical necessity.

It has often been said that the democratic form of government is the best, but also the most difficult. After surveying the ways of the totalitarian States one feels more convinced than ever that the effort to overcome the difficulties is distinctly worth continuing.

CHAPTER IX

WAR AND PEACE

THE CHIEF FACTORS

THERE is much in the teachings and methods of
Mussolini and Hitler to justify the general foreboding
with which Fascist Italy and National Socialist Germany are viewed abroad. The Italian invasion of
Ethiopia could not but strengthen the widely-held
opinion that Fascism and National Socialism necessarily mean war. However, there are involved certain
broader issues which cannot and should not be dismissed.

The Italian campaign in Abyssinia has brought
into the foreground of public discussion a question
that has long been worrying the more thoughtful
observers of international affairs—the question of
territorial expansion. The whole complicated machinery for the collective maintenance of peace,
which since the end of the war has been built up
around the League of Nations and which has been
supplemented by innumerable non-aggression pacts,
would seem to be constructed on the assumption
that the world will continue for all time to come
without any changes in its present territorial frontiers. The only article of the Covenant that may be
interpreted as affording an opportunity for changes

is the loosely worded Article 19, which refers to the possibility of revising existing treaties and to "the consideration of international conditions whose continuance might endanger the peace of the world." Few, however, have ever suggested that Article 19 provides an escape from the *impasse,* and that its application would be likely to result in any substantial redrafting of the map of the world. This situation creates a feeling of extreme uneasiness and not infrequently gives the impression that the more one talks of peace the more one thinks of war. This feeling of uneasiness is further strengthened if one takes a glance at a map and compares the relative position of the various Powers. It has often been said that the nations of the world may be broadly divided into two groups: those "who have" and those "who have not." This refers, of course, to the size of any national territory as compared with its population, and also to the supply of essential raw materials. Of the first group, the United States, Great Britain, France and the Soviet Union are the best examples; of the second, Italy, Germany and Japan. Far less enthusiasm for the existing machinery for the maintenance of peace has been shown by the nations "who have not" than by the nations "who have." Japan has been expanding with impunity in Manchuria and China. Italy, at the time of writing, is fighting her way through the mountain wastes of Abyssinia with practically all other countries aligned against her. The eyes of the world are turned with deep anxiety and apprehension toward a Germany that is straining every nerve in a determined effort to build up a powerful war machine.

There are many who believe that the chief cause of the present international complications and international tension is the existence in certain countries of government by a dictator. "We have a new factor in Europe," declared Mr. Stanley Baldwin at Bournemouth on October 4, 1935. "We have dictatorships and we know that historically, however pacifist early stages of such forms of government may be in their intentions, a tendency has shown itself later to divert attention from domestic difficulties to external adventures." From this Mr. Baldwin drew a conclusion that could not but be pleasing to his audience—he was addressing a conference of the Conservative Party—namely, that Great Britain would have to increase her armaments in order to be in a position to fulfill her obligations under the Covenant of the League of Nations. The comments of the British press and the results of the general election of November 1935 would seem to indicate that Mr. Baldwin has the country solidly behind him.

Nevertheless, his explanation of Mussolini's East African venture—for, presumably, the Duce was one of the dictators Mr. Baldwin had in mind—can hardly be accepted as adequate and complete, although it contains an important element of truth. The patent weakness of Mr. Baldwin's argument is the omission of any reference to the great national problem of overpopulation and expansion, which the

East African expedition is attempting to solve in a manner that may be entirely wrong. It would hardly be correct to assume that Mussolini was driven into his colonial venture by domestic difficulties. I have made it clear that Italy, like many other countries, was in 1934–1935 experiencing serious economic troubles. But it is not easy to see how these difficulties could be relieved by a colonial expedition which, even in the case of complete and speedy military success, would prove an immense financial burden and, for many years to come, would involve large outlays for the development of the newly acquired territory. An undertaking of this nature can hardly be described as an attempt "to divert attention from domestic difficulties to external adventures." It must also be borne in mind that as a consequence of their very low standards of living the masses of the Italian people are not quite so susceptible to the effects of the depression as are those of countries with higher standards. Moreover, the Italians endure economic privation with seemingly inexhaustible patience.

ITALY AND ABYSSINIA

The chief elements of the situation have been outlined in earlier chapters. We already know that Italy has a territory which only at a considerable sacrifice can produce sufficient foodstuffs to feed a prolific and rapidly increasing population; that she depends almost entirely on imports for her supplies of raw materials; that the standards of living of her people are appallingly low. And we also know that Italy is now under a dictatorship which, through an elaborate network of Party agencies and a state-controlled press, has practically unlimited opportunities for influencing public opinion.

It must be remembered that the economic difficulties of Italy have been greatly intensified in the course of the last years. The shrinkage of "invisible" exports and international trade, aggravated by the overvaluation of the lira and the depreciation of the pound sterling and the dollar, has been a formidable obstacle to Italy's obtaining the foreign exchange necessary for the purchase of raw materials which, to repeat, are vital to her industry. Emigration, which used to be a safety-valve for Italian surplus population, has been practically cut off since the beginning of the depression. The 200,000 Italians or more who used to find seasonal work in France, Germany, Belgium and Switzerland have been forced by immigration restrictions to remain in idleness within the national frontiers. No reasonable person could blame other European nations or overseas countries, which are wrestling with their own problems of wide domestic unemployment, for closing their frontiers to Italian labor. But this is cold comfort to the Italians who are brought face to face with the inescapable fact that a country like theirs, which is not in a position to provide a decent living for its own people is, even more than other countries, at the mercy of uncontrollable economic forces, to say nothing of international political emergencies. The plight of Italy has not passed unnoticed. "We have always understood and well understand Italy's desire for overseas expansion . . ." said Sir Samuel Hoare in the House of Commons on July 11, 1935. "Let no one therefore in Italy . . . suggest that we are unsympathetic to Italian aspirations." But he added, of course, that the legitimacy of Italy's desire for expansion was in no way a sufficient reason for her plunging into war.

The undoubted fact of Italy's need for expansion does not in itself explain the present East African expedition. Italian peasants and workers naturally know as much about Abyssinia as do people in other countries, that is, practically nothing; the idea of embarking on the conquest of the realm of the King of Kings could never have occurred to them. This is where the responsibility of the Fascist Government begins. I have quoted, in my discussion of Fascist doctrine, excerpts from Mussolini's writings which glorify war and heroism. It is in the deserts of Abyssinia and under the tropical sun of East Africa that this creed is to receive its acid test. Some 25 years ago Mussolini was one of the most outspoken critics of the Libyan expedition and one of the leading "anti-Africanists." Since then, he has changed his mind on this subject, as he has on so many others. There may be danger in thinking and talking too much of the glory of ancient Rome. The imperial dream of the Duce is written in stone on the walls of the venerable Basilica of Maxentius

whose noble ruins stand on the Via dell'Impero, in
the very heart of the Roma Mussoliniana. His appeal to the imagination of the Italians took the form
of four maps. The first represents Rome in the
eighth century B.C., when it was merely a city; then
comes the Rome of 146 B.C., after the Punic Wars,
and third, the Roman Empire of 14 A.D., at the time
of the death of Augustus. The fourth and last map
depicts the Empire under Trajan, in 96–114 A.D. The
territories then under Roman rule did not merely
encircle the Mediterranean. They also comprised
large portions of further Europe, including all of
Spain and a good part of the British Isles and extended eastward to the Black Sea, the Caspian Sea
and the Arabian Gulf. The difference between the
first map and the last is striking indeed. What
was the purpose of this object lesson in ancient
geography?

In the late summer of 1935 no visitor to Italy who
was not completely cut off from local opinion could
possibly doubt that the Fascist Government was
finally and irrevocably committed to the East African venture. From discussions of the subject I had
with a large number of Italians drawn from every
class of society and every walk in life, from members of the cabinet to hotel servants and peasants,
it was made abundantly clear to me that there was
little feeling of enmity or ancient grudge against
Abyssinia herself. The whole expedition was held
to constitute a war of necessity: Italy was fighting
for her place in the sun. It was not imagined, of

course, in responsible circles that the conquest of
Abyssinia would solve all Italy's difficulties. But it
was believed that a new East African colony would
provide large tracts of fertile and still unoccupied
land on the upper plateau, where climatic conditions
were reported to be suitable for white colonization.
This opinion was fully corroborated by a recent and
authoritative publication of the British Royal Institute of International Affairs. The future settlers
were visualized as small farmers who would be able
to produce enough for their own needs and for the
needs of the mother country without trying to engage in competitive wheat exporting for the international market. In keeping with that romanticism
which is characteristic of every movement of the
Fascist Government the colonists were first to con-
quer the land in the best tradition of the Roman
legions, and then settle down on it under the protection of the Italian flag and the lictor's rods. It was
also believed that Abyssinia would be able to produce at least two commodities that count heavily
today among Italy's imports: cotton and coffee.
There were rumors, too, that Abyssinia contained
much mineral wealth and large deposits of oil, but
in responsible circles these reports were heavily dis-
counted.

From the very beginning the soundness of the
East African venture was open to considerable
doubt, even leaving aside the probability of international complications, which have since material-
ized to an extent no one could possibly have foreseen

in the summer of 1935. The large-scale colonization of an African territory by Europeans presented a novel and difficult problem. It would be extremely costly and, until many years had passed, could not possibly make any return on the large investment demanded. Even in one who knows nothing about colonial warfare, the mere vastness of Abyssinia and the reported difficulties of terrain and climate inspire the gravest apprehension. The Italians seemed to have a boundless confidence in their air force and the use of the most modern methods of warfare. I was told, indeed, that never before in colonial history had an expedition been undertaken with so large and well-equipped a force. But one naturally feels that these very elements of novelty might well contain the elements of danger. To a member of the Mussolini cabinet, who was good enough to grant me an interview, I stated very frankly the doubts in my mind concerning the economic and technical aspects of the East African expedition. He listened to my argument with the greatest courtesy and serenity and then asked me if I could offer Italy anything better than Abyssinia. The Fascist position was made perfectly clear: Italy needed expansion, and East Africa was the only possible outlet. I was also assured from a very high source that the purely military part of the Abyssinian campaign would be over before the end of the year. At the time of writing, in December, this all-important part of the program does not seem likely to be fulfilled.

Doubts and apprehensions such as I have expressed have naturally occurred to many Italians, but they have not been permitted to reach the masses. A most intensive campaign of propaganda in favor of the East African war has been relentlessly carried on, by both press and Fascist organizations. No nation is immune from the war psychosis, and the Latin temperament is perhaps particularly susceptible to it. The result has been that public opinion has become the victim of the most extraordinary delusions. The most striking, perhaps, was the view generally accepted in Italy in the summer of 1935 that Great Britain was a decadent nation, and that the British fleet was entirely at the mercy of the Italian air force. The irrefutable evidence of British decadence, offered virtually dozens of times, was the perfectly innocuous, if rather widely advertised resolution of the Oxford Union in which the undergraduates of England's ancient university proclaimed their decision not to fight for King and Country. It was argued in Rome from this and similar premises that when it came to a choice between Italy and England, France in her quest for European security was bound to side with the former. The developments at Geneva and the imposition of sanctions by the League must have caused a rude awakening.

But the great propaganda effort made possible by the Fascist Party's absolute control over the country has borne fruit. The war in East Africa, which had its immediate origin in the decision of the Duce, has grown into a national problem. The great masses of Italians were led to believe that practically their

very existence as a nation, as well as the safeguarding of national honor, depended on the successful issue of the campaign. Up to the beginning of
September, I think, there was no real enthusiasm
for the war except among the young, but there was a
real determination to back the Government and see
the thing through. Judging by newspaper reports
the international repercussions of the East African
adventure have not weakened this feeling, but have
made it even stronger. There must be dissenting
voices, but they are not heard.

THE LEAGUE OF NATIONS AND THE CONFLICT

On the eve of M. Laval's departure for Geneva
early in September 1935, there was a great deal of
uneasiness in French political circles over the Ethiopian situation. The Paris *Temps,* which always re-
flects the opinions of the Quai d'Orsay, said on that
occasion that the task of the French Prime Minister
consisted in maintaining Franco-British cooperation,
safeguarding Franco-Italian friendship, and solving
the Ethiopian problem without damaging the
authority of the League of Nations. It will be
agreed that this was a rather formidable assign-
ment. A student who approaches the international
phase of the Ethiopian conflict with a desire to be
objective finds himself, like M. Laval, in an unfortunate position. It is impossible to feel anything
but the deepest sympathy for Ethiopia, who is very
much in the position of the whipping boy, except

that that unhappy nation not only gets the thrash-
ing but also faces the menace of wholesale swallow-
ing by Italy. The Ethiopian delegate, Teclé Hawar-
jate, made an extremely moving appeal before the
Council of the League when he stated that the first
taste of European civilization his countrymen were
getting was their contact with Italy's powerful war
machine, and that they were being exterminated by
modern instruments of warfare the very existence
of which they never suspected. This is unfortunately
only too true, although it is also true, as it is argued
on the Italian side, that the Ethiopian Government
has decided limitations, and that the method of
bringing civilization to the natives, so rightly de-
plored by the Ethiopian delegate, is by no means
peculiar to Italy. This is indeed the way in which
civilization, under the protection of various national
flags, was introduced to not a few of the so-called
backward nations in other parts of Africa and, for
that matter, all over the world. The familiar euphe-
mism—the "white man's burden"—has a very real
counterpart in the "colored man's burden."

But all the sympathy should not go to Ethiopia
alone. I have already discussed Italy's need for
territorial expansion the legitimacy of which, to repeat, was acknowledged by Sir Samuel Hoare. And
one cannot disregard the fact that by September and
October 1935 the East African expedition was no
longer Mussolini's private war, but in the full sense
of the term a great national enterprise for the success of which millions of Italians were prepared to

make the supreme sacrifice of their lives. The Council of the League of Nations had to consider not only the factors directly involved in the Italo-Ethiopian dispute but, above all, the probable repercussions of its own decision upon the existing structure of collective security and the general course of world politics. There are good reasons for believing that it is the latter considerations that have played an exceptionally large part in framing the Council's policies. So the Council of the League also deserves sympathy in its ungrateful task.

I need not go into the details of the Geneva procedure for they are not essential to my purpose. The gist of the Italian argument at Geneva, which, I think, voiced something that is very different from the real causes of the conflict—was that Abyssinia was a barbaric country unable and unwilling to maintain its treaty obligations, and that Italy's action was taken in defense of her East African colonies. The chief argument of the League against Italy was that Italy had failed to live up to her obligations as a member, and had broken her pledge not to go to war. On October 7, 1935, the Council of the League named Italy as the aggressor and later voted economic sanctions, which were put into effect on November 18. At the present writing the iron ring of economic blockade is closing more and more tightly about her.

This unprecedented action of the League raises a number of perplexing and bewildering problems. One may well be permitted to question whether the imposition of sanctions against Italy is a step toward the maintenance of peace or, rather, a likely source of further and worse international complications. If my analysis of the character of Italy's East African venture is correct, and the three important elements in the situation are (1) the need for expansion, (2) the nature of Mussolini's action, and (3) the state of public opinion in Italy, it will appear that the sanctions deal only with the second point. They are meant as a penalty for the wrongdoing of the Italian Government and are to serve as a deterrent to other countries. This procedure might have been of some use if the League had been in a position to offer a solution for the other two points. The application of sanctions, needless to say, is no move toward meeting Italy's need for colonial expansion. If anything, it is very likely to intensify her desire for more territory by emphasizing the vulnerability of her present position. The effect of the Geneva decision, judging by press reports, has so far been to unite the country behind the Duce. Italy refuses to accept the verdict of Geneva, just as Germany refused to accept the verdict of Article 231 of the Treaty of Versailles. It is greatly to be feared that the ultimate results may not be altogether different.

The sanctity of treaties is, no doubt, the very foundation of the existing international order. But it is the contention of the Italians that they have not really violated the spirit of their obligations, because Abyssinia was not a worthy member of the League. This, however, is obviously a question for the League and not for Italy to decide. On the other hand, the non-fulfillment of agreements solemnly entered into is not confined to Italy. The recent records of practically every country that voted against Italy at Geneva—and also of those that are not represented in the League of Nations—have not been blameless in this respect. In many instances failure to live up to national promises is, of course, very different from the case of Italy now in question. Some of these breaches of contract had excellent justification. Two wrongs assuredly do not make one right, but in the absence of a rigid code of international ethics the decision as to when the repudiation of an obligation is permissible and when it is not is necessarily left to somewhat arbitrary interpretation. And interpretation varies within an extraordinarily wide range, from capital to capital, from year to year, and even from month to month.

In early December 1935 the military effects of the sanctions were still highly uncertain. They have undoubtedly added greatly to Italy's difficulties. But so far they have failed to stop the war, and it is by no means obvious that they will not actually prolong it. The economic consequences are much clearer. They will bring infinite misery to the hard-working and sadly tried Italians. The already humble incomes of peasants and workers will be further cut down and their frugal meals will be made even more frugal. Between the apostles of national solidarity and Roman tradition, on the one hand, and the champions of international morality, on the other, their fate is dark indeed. Other nations will be affected in a similar way, although in lesser degree. The prohibition of trade with Italy will necessarily bring in its wake increased unemployment in exporting countries, and will further hamper international trade, on the expansion of which so many of us have believed the recovery of the world largely depends. It will also undoubtedly intensify that desire for economic self-sufficiency that has been one of the curses of the world, especially since the war. For the international scene is subject to rapid and dramatic changes. Only a few short months ago Mussolini was considered by many distinguished minds on both sides of the Atlantic to be one of Europe's greatest statesmen and a real friend of peace, his own eulogies of war notwithstanding. This evanescence of international reputations has been dramatically brought to the attention of the members of the League by the personal tragedy of the Italian delegate, Baron Aloisi. A year ago, and as late as the spring of 1935, he was one of the League's most outstanding figures. It was "Baron Aloisi's Committee" that handled for the Council the thorny Saar question. The most extravagant praise was showered in those days upon the distinguished Italian delegate. In the autumn of 1935 Baron Aloisi fought a losing battle in the defense of his country's case at Geneva. He spoke amidst icy silence and left the tribune without a single handclap. Who can say whose turn will come next? The inevitable conclusion would seem to be that one must be prepared for the worst.

These and similar considerations could not have been ignored by the members of the League's Council and Assembly. They reached their decision against Italy with heavy hearts and in full recognition of the fact that every country will have to carry its share of the burden. But while their earnestness cannot be questioned, the wisdom of the decision itself is open to doubt. If one could at least be sure that the privations resulting from the application of the sanctions will really serve the ultimate cause of peace and international morality! The latter, however, as I have already pointed out, is open to innumerable interpretations. And, in the last analysis, the maintenance of peace is not so much a question of the perfection of written agreements and the number of signatures attached to them, as of the sincere desire of the nations to live up to the spirit of these agreements. Italy believes, rightly or wrongly, that she has been the victim of the most odious form of discrimination by the League. In the best Roman tradition the events of the fateful day of November 18, when the sanctions were put into effect, have been made a part of the official record of the Eternal City through the unveiling of an appropriately inscribed marble tablet. The Italians are not likely to forget that date for many years to come, just as the Germans have not forgotten the Versailles *Diktat*. "It is difficult to give an adequate idea of the fierce, burning resentment Italians feel against the sanctionist countries . . ." writes the Rome correspondent of the *New York Times,* Arnaldo Cortesi. "Apparently staid, well-balanced men fairly froth at the mouth when they speak of Italy's allies in the World War. They feel that they are the victims of the greatest injustice that has been done since the beginning of the world, and they hate the perpetrators of it." There is also in every country, especially in France, strong opposition to the enforcement of the sanctions. This opposition is bound to grow stronger as the pinch due to their enforcement is felt more and more. The resulting situation cannot but be fraught with the gravest risk of social unrest, and it augurs ill for that spirit of good will and desire for international cooperation that is the only real safeguard of international peace.

The chief weakness of the steps taken at Geneva is perhaps the fact that they are concerned merely with the desire "to stop the war," and contain no provision whatsoever for correcting the situation that brought about the conflict. This may be inherent in the very nature of the League, which must proceed in accordance with the provisions of its Covenant. The basic problems, however, were brought to the attention of the League's Assembly on September 11, 1935, in a notable speech by Sir Samuel Hoare. The British Secretary for Foreign Affairs discussed the question of raw materials and recognized its importance, though he expressed the opinion that the significance attached by many governments to the political control of sources of raw materials appeared to him exaggerated. "The view of His Majesty's Government," said Sir Samuel, "is that the problem is economic rather than political and territorial. It is the fear of monopoly—of the withholding of essential colonial raw materials that is causing alarm." He suggested the holding of an inquiry to study the question, and proposed that "the emphasis in the terms of reference should fall upon the free distribution of such raw materials among the industrial countries which require them, so that all fear of exclusion or monopoly may be removed once and for all." He added that "such an inquiry needs calm and dispassionate consideration, and calm and dispassionate consideration is impossible in an atmosphere of war and threatenings of war." The fact that the Government of Great Britain expressed its willingness to participate in such an inquiry was certainly a significant and novel departure which may prove to be the first step in the right direction. By a great part of the French and English press Sir Samuel's speech was acclaimed as a model of lucidity and as representing a new factor of immense importance in international affairs.

The reason for this enthusiastic reception has always been to me something of a mystery, especially since Sir Samuel himself admitted that his impression is that "there is no question in present circumstances of any colony withholding its raw materials from any prospective purchaser. On the contrary, the trouble is that they cannot be sold at *remunera-*

tive prices." This last statement of Sir Samuel gives a very accurate description of the situation. The real problem is not that of monopolies of raw materials, but of the inability of the nations in need of these materials to pay for them. We have seen that precisely this inability is one of Germany's greatest troubles and was one of the greatest troubles of Italy before the application of the sanctions. It will come up again the moment the sanctions are removed. The consideration of national safety in time of war also should not be overlooked. But if this is the situation, what is the meaning of the proposal of the British Government? In its present form it means hardly anything, and one may only hope that if and when the proposed inquiry is made it may be transferred from the purely illusory ground assigned to it by Sir Samuel to a more concrete and practical one, that of the redistribution of colonial mandates among those Powers who feel that the limited area of their national territory is a real bar to their progress and development.

THE CASE OF GERMANY

Italy is, of course, not the only country in this position. Although Germany did not participate in the Geneva discussion of the Ethiopian crisis she was certainly present in the minds of the delegates. It needs no special political acumen or profound knowledge of the European situation to perceive that, but for her deep concern over recent developments in Germany, the attitude of France toward sanctions would have been even more lukewarm, and her cooperation with Great Britain less enthusiastic than it proved to be in the autumn of 1935. The French press leaves no possible doubt that the Ethiopian crisis in itself is regarded as a very secondary matter, and that what really counts is the preservation of the existing machinery of insurance treaties and collective arrangements for the maintenance of peace, so that it may be used against Germany in case France finds herself in conflict with her eastern neighbor.

The question that naturally arises is whether France is justified in her fears of aggression on the part of Germany.

Many of the aspects of the National Socialist Government are anything but reassuring. It will be remembered that Hitler, no less than Mussolini, is a firm believer in war as the supreme law of humanity. The whole organization of the National Socialist Party and of the National Socialist State, even more than that of Fascist Italy, is imbued with the martial spirit. Men and women, half-grown boys and girls, and mere children spend much of their time in military exercises or on the drilling ground. There are uniforms and marching columns everywhere. A decree of the Chancellor in November 1935 declared that practically the entire population must be held to be members of the Nation's military forces and liable to call to the service at any time. In

March 1935 Hitler officially repudiated the disarmament clauses of the Versailles Treaty. This action, however, was not without justification. The summer of 1935 saw much bitter criticism in the French press of Britain's insistence upon the application of sanctions against Italy since England did not consider such action against Germany after her repudiation of the disarmament provisions.[1] Replying to this criticism the London *Times,* which on several occasions has spoken of the Hitler Government in terms of unusual severity, said editorially on August 29: "They [the French] must remember that in the matter of rearmament Germany at least waited very patiently for ten years while the League tried to solve the problem. The right of equality had long been acknowledged, in principle; and only after many years had passed without its concession in practice did Germany take the matter into her own hands in violation of the treaty, of which, in that respect, she had never admitted the validity." The position of Germany as the only great Power with limitations upon her armaments in the midst of nations that continued to strengthen their own armed forces was an obvious anomaly. It was a situation that was not meant even by the Treaty of Versailles to be made permanent. Its disappearance, I think, should be welcome because this inequality was one of the sources of the most extreme and aggressive form of German nationalism.

[1] This Franco-British controversy regarding obligations imposed by international agreements is a good example of the extreme latitude in interpretation to which I have referred.

But even if this is admitted—and I am aware that there are many who will here disagree with me—the fact nevertheless remains that some of the doctrines, and especially the methods and the spirit of the National Socialist movement, cannot but create a feeling of great uneasiness and apprehension. Hitler has spoken much of peace in the course of the last months. His relations with Poland have been greatly improved. The Chancellor has declared that after the return of the Saar to Germany there were no more territorial questions between Germany and France. Peace, indeed, has been the keynote of official German pronouncement for the last two years. I was surprised to find how little interest the minor officials of the National Socialist Party took in international problems, including those of Germany's "bleeding borders." Unfortunately public opinion in Germany, probably to an even more marked degree than in Fascist Italy, is susceptible to sudden and complete revisal under the pressure of Party organizations and the controlled press. We have seen how the inherently peace-loving and easy-going Italians have been brought to the highest pitch of militaristic exaltation, and this for a cause which in itself could hardly make any broad appeal. The experience is instructive and the possibility of its repetition in Germany is by no means excluded.

In the case of Germany, however, just as in that of Italy, the element of potential danger to peace is not due merely to the character and methods of the present Government. There is also the fundamental

and inescapable fact that Germany has need of raw
materials and of freedom to expand. While, at the
end of the war, Italy at least added to her territory
in Europe, Germany at the same time lost not only
her colonial empire but also large sections of her
homeland. Hitler, in *Mein Kampf,* is very critical
of colonial expansion. He goes so far as to advocate
the complete abandonment of colonial ambitions
and even of the navy, this with a view to obtaining
an alliance with Great Britain. His aim is the conquest of new territory in eastern Europe and its
settlement by people of German blood. But these
statements in *Mein Kampf* do not seem to represent
the attitude of the German Government of today.
The Chancellor and many of the National Socialist
leaders have frequently insisted upon the necessity
of the restoration of Germany's colonies as the best
way out of her present economic difficulties. Dr.
Schacht has for years been consistently and untir-
ingly giving voice to the same conviction. In his
address at the Leipzig Fair of 1935 he advanced the
argument that the return of her colonies to the
Reich would, by reducing the volume of raw materials that Germany has to purchase abroad, relieve
exchange difficulties; he maintained that this would,
in turn, increase the likelihood that Germany's foreign creditors would receive what was due them.
This was presumably an invitation to the creditors
to use their good offices in favor of Germany's cause.

The National Socialists have taken great pains to
make clear that such colonial expansion as they

have in mind must be accomplished by peaceful means. In this they are probably sincere, at least for the present. But how can one be sure of Germany's attitude when her program of rearmament shall have been completed? The very existence of the problem contains a latent element of conflict which cannot and should not be ignored.

We are thus led to the perhaps not very new or original conclusion that the best method of preventing international conflicts is a policy that is based on the recognition of other nations' legitimate needs. To get the various nations to agree upon what constitutes this legitimate need is not an easy matter and to make them agree upon the manner in which such need can best be met is even more difficult. There is no real assurance that concessions would not lead to new and more extensive demands. Even should some nations show the fullest desire to cooperate there is no certainty, of course, that this would be met in the same spirit by other nations. Nevertheless the attempt should be made. For the only alternative is the road that led Italy to sacrifice the flower of her manhood on the battlefields of Abyssinia.

BIBLIOGRAPHY [1]

Books and Pamphlets

Annuario statistico italiano, anno 1935—XIII, Rome, 1925.

ARMSTRONG, HAMILTON FISH, *Hitler's Reich*, New York, 1933.

BARAVELLI, G. C., *Integral Land Reclamation in Italy*, Rome, 1935.

BARAVELLI, G. C., *Policy of Public Works under the Fascist Régime*, Rome, 1935.

BOTTAI, GIUSEPPE, *Esperienza Corporativa* (1929–1935), Florence, 1935.

BOTTAI, GIUSEPPE, *Le Corporazioni*, Milan, 1935.

Commissariato Generale dell'Emigrazione, L'emigrazione italiana dal 1910 al 1923, Rome, 1926.

Confederazione Fascista dei Lavoratori del Commercio, Azione sindacale contro la disoccupazione, Rome, 1935.

DAESCHNER, L., *Die Deutsche Arbeitsfront*, Munich, 1934.

Deutsche Arbeitsfront—N. S. G. Kraft durch Freude, Schönheit der Arbeit, Berlin, 1935.

Die deutsche Erzeugungsschlacht, Berlin, 1935.

FANNO, MARCO, *Introduzione allo studio della teoria economica del corporativismo*, Padua, 1935.

FANTINI, ODDONE, *Stato e lavoro*, Rome, 1928.

FEDER, GOTTFRIED, *Das Programm der N. S. D. A. P. und seine weltanschaulichen Grundgedanken*, Munich, 1934.

[1] Only the more important publications consulted in the preparation of this volume are included in the lists.

277

FINER, HERMAN, *Mussolini's Italy*, London, 1935.

Flugschriften des Reichsnährstandes, Aufbau und Durchführung der landwirtschaftlichen Marktordnung, Berlin, 1935.

FRAUENDORFER, MAX, *Ständischer Aufbau*, Berlin, 1935.

GANGEMI, LELLO, *La politica economica e finanziaria del Governo Fascista*, Bologna, 1924.

GANGEMI, LELLO, *Pressione tributaria, produzione e scambi internazionali*, Florence, 1935.

HAIDER, CARMEN, *Capital and Labor under Fascism*, New York, 1930.

HEIDEN, KONRAD, *A History of National Socialism*, London, 1934.

HEISS, FRIEDRICH, *Deutschland zwischen Nacht und Tag*, Berlin, 1934.

HIERL, KONSTANTIN, *Grundsätzliches zur Arbeitsdienstpflicht*, Berlin, 1934.

HITLER, ADOLF, *Mein Kampf*, Munich, 1933.

HITLER, ADOLF, *Liberty, Art, Nationhood*, Berlin, 1935.

HOCHE, WERNER, *Die Gesetzgebung des Kabinetts Hitler*, Berlin, 1933–1935.

HOOVER, CALVIN B., *Germany Enters the Third Reich*, New York, 1933.

HÖVEL, PAUL, *Grundfragen deutscher Wirtschaftspolitik*, Berlin, 1935.

Institut International d'Agriculture, Les conditions de l'agriculture mondiale en 1933–1934, Rome, 1935.

Istituto Coloniale Fascista, Annuario delle colonie italiane e paesi vicini, anno XIII, Rome, 1935.

Istituto Nazionale Fascista di Cultura, Legislatione e ordinamento sindacale corporativo, Rome, 1934.

Istituto Nazionale Fascista per gli Scambi con l'Estero, Autorizzazione ad importazioni in compensazione privata, Rome, 1935.

Istituto Nazionale Fascista per gli Scambi con l'Estero, Dati statistici sul commercio estero italiano nel quinquennio 1930–1934, Rome, 1935.

Istituto Nazionale Fascista per gli Scambi con l'Estero, Nuovo regime delle importazioni e delle compensazioni private, Rome, 1935.

JACOB, ERNST GERHARD (editor), *Kolonialpolitisches Quellenheft,* Berlin, 1935.

JOHAE, WERNER, *Das Reichserbhofgesetz,* Berlin, 1934.

KÖHLER, BERNHARD, *Des Führers Wirtschaftspolitik,* Munich, 1935.

KÖHLER, BERNHARD, *Wirtschaft und Sozialismus,* Berlin, 1935.

KRETZSCHMANN, H., und EDEL, FRITZ, *Der Weg zum Arbeitsdienst,* Berlin, 1934.

VON LEERS, JOHANN, *Kurzgefasste Geschichte des Nationalsozialismus,* Leipzig, 1933.

LESSONA, ALESSANDRO, *Realizzazioni e propositi del colonialismo italiano,* Rome, 1935.

LOEWENSTEIN, PRINCE HUBERTUS, *The Tragedy of a Nation, Germany 1918–1934,* New York, 1934.

LUDWIG, EMIL, *Talks with Mussolini,* London, 1932.

MAGRI, FRANCESCO, *La bonifica delle paludi pontine e l'Opera Nazionale per i Combattenti,* Milan, 1933.

MARPICATI, ARTURO, *Il Partito Fascista,* Milan, 1935.

DE MICHELIS, GIUSEPPE, *La corporazione nel mondo,* Milan, 1934.

Ministère de l'Agriculture et des Forêts, Les progrès de l'agriculture italienne en régime fasciste, Rome, 1934.

Minister dell'Agriculture et des Foreste, La bonifica integrale, Rome, 1935.

Ministero delle Corporazioni Elementi di ordinamento corporativo, Rome, 1935.

Ministero delle Finanze, Il bilancio dello Stato dal 1913–1914 al 1929–1930 e la finanza fascista a tutto l'anno VIII, Rome, 1931.

Ministero delle Finanze, Il bilancio e il conto generale del patrimonio dello Stato per l'esercizio finanziario 1930–1931, Rome, 1932.

Ministero delle Finanze, Il bilancio e il conto generale del patrimonio dello Stato per l'esercizio finanziario 1931–1932, Rome, 1933.

Ministero delle Finanze, *La finanza statale dell'anno XI (esercizio 1932–1933)*, Rome, 1934.

Ministero delle Finanze, *La finanza statale dell'anno XII (esercizio 1933–1934)*, Rome, 1935.

MISSIROLI, MARIO, *L'Italia d'oggi*, Bologna, 1932.

MÖNCKMEIER, OTTO (editor), *Jahrbuch für national-sozialistische Wirtschaft*, Stuttgart-Berlin, 1935.

MORTARA, GIORGIO, *L'Italia e l'economia corporativa di fronte alla crisi economica mondiale*, Rome, 1934.

MORTARA, GIORGIO (editor), *Prospettive economiche*, Milan, 1924–1934.

MOTZ, KARL, *Blut und Boden*, Berlin, 1934.

MUSSOLINI, BENITO, *Diritti e interessi dell'Italia in Africa Orientale*, Rome, 1935.

MUSSOLINI, BENITO, *Fascism: Doctrine and Institutions*, Rome, 1935.

MUSSOLINI, BENITO, *Four Speeches on the Corporate State*, Rome, 1935.

MÜLLER-BRADENBURG, *Was ist Arbeitsdienst? Was soll er?* Leipzig, 1934.

NIKISCH, A., *Das Gesetz zur Ordnung der Nationalen Arbeit*, Leipzig, 1934.

NORLIN, GEORGE, *Fascism and Citizenship*, Chapel Hill, 1934.

Opera Balilla anno XI, Milan, 1933.

L'Opera Balilla nell'anno XII, Rome, 1935.

Opera Balilla, VIII leva fascista, Milan, 1934.

Opera Balilla, Rivoluzione Fascista, Rome, 1934.

Opera Nazionale per i Combattenti, *La bonifica e la trasformazione fondiaria dell'Agro Pontino*, Rome, 1935.

Opera Nazionale per i Combattenti, *Il contratto di mezzadria per i coloni dell'Agro Pontino*, Rome, 1933.

L'organisation syndicale et corporative italienne, Rome, 1935.

Organisation der deutschen Arbeitsfront und der N. S. Gemeinschaft Kraft durch Freude, Berlin, 1934.

PARINI, PIERO, *Gli italiani nel mondo*, Milan, 1935.

PITIGLIANI, FAUSTO, *The Italian Corporative State*, New York, 1934.

RAUE, ERNST, *Beiträge zur neuen Staats- und Wirtschaftsauffassung in Deutschland und Italien*, Berlin, 1934.

Les réalisations et le developpement de l'Œuvre Nationale Dopolavoro, Borgo San Dalmazzo, 1933.

Rechenschaftsbericht der deutschen Arbeitsfront, Berlin, 1935.

Reichs-Kredit-Gesellschaft, Deutschland's Wirtschaftliche Entwicklung, 1933, 1934, 1934–1935, 1935, Berlin.

REINHARDT, FRITZ, *Die Arbeitsschlacht der Reichsregierung*, Berlin, 1933.

Relazioni e proposte della commissione per lo studio delle riforme constituzionali, Florence, 1932.

Richtlinien für die Vertrauensratswahlen, 1935.

RÖPKE, WILHELM, *German Commercial Policy*, London, 1934.

ROSENSTOCK-FRANCK, L., *L'économie corporative fasciste en doctrine et en fait*, Paris, 1934.

Royal Institute of International Affairs, *Abyssinia and Italy*, London, 1935.

Royal Institute of International Affairs, *The Economic and Financial Position of Italy*, London, 1935.

SCHACHT, HJALMAR, Speeches, 1930–1935.

SCHACHT, HJALMAR, and others, *Deutschland und die Wirtschaft*, Berlin, 1935.

SCHNEIDER, HERBERT W., *Making of the Fascist State*, New York, 1928.

SCHWEIGART, HANS ADALBERT, *Bauerntum und Marktordnung*, 1934.

SERING, MAX, *Deutsche Agrarpolitik*, Leipzig, 1934.

SERPIERI, A., *La legge sulla bonifica integrale nel quinto anno di applicazione*, Rome, 1935.

SOMBART, WERNER, *Deutscher Sozialismus*, Berlin, 1934.

SPIRITO, UGO, *Capitalismo e corporativismo*, Florence, 1934.

Statistisches Jahrbuch für das Deutsche Reich, Berlin, 1934.

TOYNBEE, ARNOLD J., *Survey of International Affairs, 1933*, London, 1934.

VITO, FRANCESCO, *L'economia corporativa nazionale nell'ambito del mercato mondiale*, Milan, 1935.

VITO, FRANCESCO, and others, *Economia corporativa*, Milan, 1935.

VOLPE, GIOACCHINO, *History of the Fascist Movement*, Rome, 1935.

Was wir erreicht haben und was wir erreichen werden! Berlin, 1934.

Winter-Hilfswerk des deutschen Volkes, 1933–1934.

Work of the National Fascist Institute of Social Insurance, Rome, 1935.

Periodicals

Business and Financial Reports, published by the Association of Italian Corporations and the Fascist Confederation of Industrialists, Rome.

Der deutsche Volkswirt, Berlin.

The Economist, London.

Foreign Policy Reports, New York.

Die Form, Zeitschrift für Gestaltende Arbeit, Berlin.

Gazzetta Ufficiale del Regno d'Italia, Rome.

Institut International d'Agriculture, Bulletin mensuel de renseignements économique et sociaux, Rome.

International Conciliation, published by the Carnegie Endowment for International Peace, New York.

News Notes on Fascist Corporations, published by the Ministry of Corporations, Rome.

Odal, Monatsschrift für Blut und Boden, Berlin.

Raccolta delle leggi e decreti del Regno d'Italia, Rome.

Riforma Sociale, Turin.

Reichsgesetzblatt, Berlin.

Siedlung und Wirtschaft, Berlin.

Sindacati e Corporazioni, Rome.

Vierteljahrshefte zur Konjunkturforschung, Berlin.

La Vita Economica Italiana, Rome and Padua.

Weltwirtschaftliches Archiv, Jena.

Wirtschaft und Statistik, Berlin.

Wochenbericht des Instituts für Konjunkturforschung, Berlin.

INDEX

285

Matteotti, 22.
Maxentius, Basilica of, 257.
Mazzini, 8.
Messagero, Il, 170.
Militia, Fascist. *See* Fascist Party.
Ministry of Corporations, 83-84, 90, 94-95, 124-125.
Ministry of Propaganda, 100, 112, 231.
Monopolies, 184-185, 204.
Montecitorio. *See* Parliament, Italian.
Munich *Putsch*, 40-41.
Mussolini, Benito, expulsion from Socialist Party, 5, 9; organization of the Milan *fascio*, 10; attitude before 1921, 10; his following in 1921, 11; and the Socialists, 11; his program in 1921, 12; on the Party, 13; alarmed by brutalities, 14; offers to resign from the Fascist Party, 14; and party membership, 15; editor of *Avanti*, 16; on monarchy, 17; on Parliament, 18; forms cabinet, 18, 47; on democracy, 18-19, 59; devotion of Militia to, 20; on election law, 21; and Parliament, 21-22; and the Matteotti murder, 22; and Fascist opinion, 25-26; on the future of the Chamber of Deputies, 26; as leader, 37; influence of, 45; master of Italy, 53; on Fascist philosophy, 56; influenced by, 58; on the supremacy of the State, 59; on Roman tradition, 62-63; on freedom, 65; on Roman Prussianism, 66; on duty, 66; on class struggle, 67-68, 118; on dignity of labor, 71; on war, 72-74, 257; claim to spiritual leadership, 75; and self-criticism, 78; on economic liberalism, 85; and

the agreement of Palazzo Chigi, 87; definition of corporations, 91; on the corporate system, 95; on the Corporate State, 96; association with labor, 121; champion of labor, 127; and reduction of unemployment, 129; and labor, 135; on land and the farmers, 155; proclaims the "Battle of the wheat," 169; on the lira, 197; on taxation, 202; prophet of Fascism, 231-232; and the Holy See, 241-242; and anti-Semitism, 244; admired and denounced, 248; and the East African campaign, 254; anti-Africanist, 257; and colonial expansion, 257-258; held as friend of peace, 267.

National Association for Land Reclamation, 165.
National Council of Corporations, 26, 85, 90, 93-94.
National income, 217.
National Socialist Cell Organization, 136, 139.
National Socialist Party, organization of, 37; program of, 38-39, 66, 118; effects of Allied policy on, 34-35; S.A. (*Sturm-Abteilung*), 39-40, 43, 46, 190, 228-229, 240; outlawed, 40; *bloc* with German People's Party, 40-41; first congress of, 40; reorganization of, 41; and Reichstag elections of 1924 and 1928, 41; and the Young Plan, 41; and the Reichstag elections of 1930, 42; expected decline of, 42; effect of unemployment on, 43; supported by young people, 44-45; and the proprietor class, 45; S.S. (*Schutz-Stauffel*), 46, 60, 80, 190, 233, 240, 246; and the

Augsburg Seminary
Library
WITHDRAWN